GOD UNBOUND

An Evangelical Reconsiders Tradition in Search of Truth

CHAD BAHL

SacraSage

Copyright © 2016 by Chad Bahl and SacraSage Press

All rights reserved. This book or any portion thereof may not be reproduced or used in any manner whatsoever without the express written permission of the publisher except for the use of brief quotations in a book review or scholarly journal.

First Edition: August 2016
Second Edition: January 2022
Print ISBN 978-1-948609-47-0
Ebook ISBN 978-1-948609-48-7

Printed in the United States of America

Library of Congress Cataloguing-in-Publication Data

God Unbound: An Evangelical Reconsiders Tradition in Search of Truth / Chad Bahl

It amazed the members of the Council to see how bold Peter and John were and to learn that they were ordinary men of no education. They realized then that they had been companions of Jesus.

—Acts 4:13

TABLE OF CONTENTS

Acknowledgements xiii

Preface xv

Chapter 1: How Hellenism Poisoned the Well 1
    What is Hellenism? 2
    Affirming a Relational God 9
    Immutability 9
    Impassibility 13
    Existential Implications-Why does it matter? 14

Chapter 2: How God Ordained Free Choice 15
    History of the Calvinist-Arminian Controversy 16
    "Determining" What is Right 20
    The Case for Determinism 20
    An Answer to the Calvinist View of Romans
    Chapter 9 23
    Biblical Argument for Free Choice 24
    Foreknowledge and Freedom 25

No Time, No Problem. 29

Existential Implications—Why does it matter?. 30

Chapter 3: The Problem of the Problem of Pain 31

Finding Comfort in Determinism. 34

The Culpability of Allowing 36

God looks like Jesus 37

Offering Genuine Comfort. 39

Chapter 4: Is Eternal Suffering for the Masses? 41

The Philosophy of Eternal Suffering 41

Origin of the Traditional View 44

On the Natural Mortality of the Soul. 45

Problem Passages. 48

Chapter 5: Incorporating Modern Science into
Theology. 53

The Debate from Darwin to Date 54

Adam: The man, the myth... 57

The Eye of the Storm 59

A Truly Dynamic Argument. 61

What Difference Does It Make?. 63

Chapter 6: The Importance of Avoiding Bibliolatry 65

The Nature of the Battle 66

Is the Bible God-Inspired? 69

    Mode of Inspiration 71

    What is bibliolatry?............................... 72

    So what should our response be? 73

Chapter 7: Escaping Evangelical Elitism 75

    Jesus, the Way the Truth 75

    Seekers not Targets 76

    A Wideness of Grace 78

    A Relational Approach 82

Chapter 8: Conclusion - The Role of Theology in
Modern Discourse 85

    #1 Your beliefs about God come from somewhere,
often not the Bible 86

    #2 Theology allows us to reconcile belief and
action 87

    #3 We become more adept at sharing our faith 87

    #4 God finds joy in those who seek after Him 88

    #5 Our own wonderment is deepened. 89

    In the end... 90

References 91

ACKNOWLEDGEMENTS

In 1994, five theologians (Clark Pinnock, Richard Rice, John Sanders, William Hasker and David Basinger) collaborated to write a book titled "The Openness of God: A Biblical Challenge to the Traditional Understanding of God." In it, they outlined a systematic view of God, christened by Rice "Open Theology." It was intended to be a challenge to "compatibilism," or the idea that human free will and divine determinism can coexist, and hopefully it would be a better response than the philosophically and logically unsustainable "Arminian incompatibilist" view of divine governance.[1] It is to this book and these authors that I owe a debt of thanks for challenging me to reconsider my "model of God."

Countless books read, much thought, many conversations, a few debates, and several years later, I now feel like I have a unique perspective to offer my fellow evangelicals. If I have done anything correctly in the following pages, I will have contributed to the ongoing dialogue of divine providence a fraction of what these men have and several of them continue to do.

PREFACE

I'm no scholar. I don't have a degree in theology and at times, I don't even consider myself to be that good at "being a Christian". As Paul so eloquently put it, "I was shown mercy so that in me, the worst of sinners, Christ Jesus might display his immense patience."[1] I am not a church leader and I have no pedigree of novels or biblical commentaries written. At the end of the day, I am a disciple of Christ and I desire nothing more than for others to know the gracious, loving, intimate God that I have come to know over the years.

I have my doctorate in the sciences and have always held firmly to the notion that true, actionable faith must be grounded in *fact versus fable*. In other words, if I can't give a "ready defense"[2] of what I believe, how can I expect to not be the "ship tossed by a wave" that James warned of in his epistle?[3] Similarly, if the very foundations of my beliefs aren't firm, how can I possibly be the ambassador Christ calls me to be?[4] It is past time to distinguish the *truths of God from the claims of history*, and it is to this end that I felt the need to pen this book.

At the onset, I want to make clear that I consider myself an evangelical Christian. I affirm the Trinity, the inspiration of Scripture, and that salvation is by God's grace and through faith in the death and resurrection of Jesus Christ. Only in the spirit of correction and conversation—not criticism—toward my evangelical brethren do I approach the topics at hand.

Further, this book is not an indictment. It is not an indictment of past leaders of the faith. Many champions of Christianity have expressed views that are the polar opposite of those espoused in the proceeding chapters. However, foresight is limited and hindsight, as they say, "is 20/20." We can't possibly assume we knew all there was to know about God pre-1994,[5] and we should always allow room to correct the mistakes of the past. In the generations to come, I would hope theologians will offer even more fresh insights to the character of the God we serve than those offered here.

Neither is this book an indictment of current leaders of the Christian faith, that would consider themselves the "theological majority."[6] Because we have limited resources, the study of theology always leaves plenty of room for disagreement. I would just hope this book offers the reader a compelling alternative to remove the barriers that I have seen built for many intellectuals to come to a saving faith in the Creator of Science and Reason.

This book is a call to believers to reconsider, or perhaps even consider for the first time, what we believe to be true about the nature of God. More importantly, it is a call to consider the *implications* of what we believe. We must be willing, if appropriate, to be the oar that rights a misdirected boat.

David Basinger, in his book "The Case for Free Will Theism," speaks out against what he calls "Bunker Theology."[7] Too often, once we have formulated a view of the divine, we only approach our reading of the Bible in such a way that seeks to support those views, however incorrect they may be. If a passage seems to contradict our way of thinking, we assume there must be an alternative explanation: "perhaps that's not really what the original text actually says." Or we just chalk up the apparent contradiction to the inexplicable "mysteries of God." I would hope, for myself, to never feel so confident in my theology of God as to not be willing to correct a wrong view once presented with compelling evidence. I hope the reader would approach this book with the same humility.

I recognize this sort of reframing isn't always the easiest approach to theological study. Being willing to alter what we believe about God can sometimes feel like acknowledging that we never truly knew God in the first place. As Clark Pinnock appropriately put it, "…the reconsidering of one's model of God [can] be a delicate issue… it may feel as if, when a familiar way of thinking about God is questioned, God himself is lost or has become distant."[8] This doesn't have to stay the case. As he goes on to state, "But the experience of re-conceptualizing can be positive. After the initial anxiety of rethinking, one will find God again in a fresh way around the next bend in the reflective road." The implications of a ship as large as the Evangelical Church propagating an errant view of its captain are intimidating to consider. Especially since, by definition, its goal is for those not yet on the boat to board and submit to His command!

While I'm not a theologian by profession, everyone who loves God and desires to know Him is a practitioner of theological study. The key question is, "from where does your view of God come?" I would expect most followers of the faith to glibly answer, "The Bible, of course." To some it seems like a rhetorical question, but is it really?

Most Christians would have a hard time disagreeing with the following statements:

- **God is unchanging**.
- **Nothing is impossible for God**.
- **God is timeless**.
- **God is in control**.
- **Everything happens for a reason**.
- **Evolution and faith cannot co-exist**.
- **Hell is the place where bad people go**.

I'd say at best, these views are extra-biblical and at worst, harmful and destructive to the mission of the evangelical faith. My point is the reader most likely believes to be true the characteristics of God *they were taught* or that are consistent with the tradition of faith from which they came. My objective in this book is to challenge tradition in search of truth. My hope is for the reader to enter that journey with me.

CHAPTER 1

How Hellenism Poisoned the Well

What is the formula for a perfect God? If there was such a formula, where would we find it? Of course, the perfect God must be "perfect," but what precisely does that mean? What attributes must be ascribed to such a Being in order to fulfill our expectations?

These are timeless questions, and eminent men have attempted to answer them for centuries. Of course, the Bible has much to say about who God is:

*God is **Holy.** (Isaiah 6:3)
*God is **Light.** (1 John 1:5)
*God is **Love.** (1 John 4:8)
*God is **Compassionate**. (Lam 3:22-23)
*God is **Just**. (Psalm 7:11)

Hundreds of additional verses can be added to those above, but what about our view of the divine might be extra-biblical? This chapter will demonstrate that the traditional view of the Christian God did not develop in a bubble. Many of the great thinkers and philosophers during the development of the early church were influenced by the culture and traditions of the time, particularly those of Hellenism. These influences have pervaded modern theological discourse. From academia to the pulpit, the philosophers of Hellenism have driven the direction of the doctrine of God, perhaps more so than the Bible itself.

What is Hellenism?

In his book "Hellenism and Christianity," Friedlander defines Hellenism as the "dissolution of racial, tribal or national particularism," and the "universal spread of Greek culture, philosophy, ethics, language, and religion."[1] Simply put, Hellenism was the attempt by the Greeks to create one unified set of thoughts, beliefs, and practices amongst a pluralistic society. The spread of Hellenism was chiefly accomplished during the reign of Alexander the Great (356-324 BC), and Hellenism's influence survives into modern times through the vessel of some of history's greatest thinkers. It is these philosophers who have unwittingly contributed more to the modern view of the Christian God than, at times, the canon of Scripture.

Socrates (469-399 BC)

Perhaps the most influential philosopher in history, the teachings of Socrates have been widely acknowledged as bringing about a turning point in philosophical study and a key to the development of Hellenistic thought. No longer was *the natural* the focus of attention, but Socrates turned thought and responsibility towards *the individual*. His teachings were so against contemporary ways of thinking that the tensions he created culminated in his forced suicide, ultimately making him one of the most influential martyrs of all time. Socrates did not leave behind any writings. What is most notable about him is the lineage of loyal followers that claim him as their philosophical mentor.[2]

Plato (429-347 BC)

As a student of Socrates, Plato is considered perhaps Greece's greatest teacher/philosopher. Socrates' influence shaped Plato's destiny and his untimely death is thought to be the turning point at which Plato decided to make his life's mission to carry on the path set out by his mentor.

Plato took on the technique of *dialogue* as not only his writing style of choice but also as the best way he knew of arriving at truth. Several of these *dialogues*, including *The Republic, Laws,* and *Timaeus,* have been accredited with guiding the philosophical thought of both secularists and theologians throughout the centuries. Many of the concepts he introduced have survived to present day.

Widely considered the centering principle of Platonic thought is his *theory of ideas*. For the reader, ideas are products of our thinking, subsequently formed after the firing of hundreds of thousands of neurons. For Plato, ideas were the ultimate form of reality. According to Ferguson, Plato thought that "ideas [are] neither physical nor mental; they are outside space and time." Ideas are real, and "…the physical world is but a poor imitation."[3] Ferguson gives the example of a perfect circle. In the world of the idea, a circle is perfect, but in reality, a perfect circle cannot be found.

No personal God exists in the Platonic world view. Perhaps the closest Plato comes is his view that the "ultimate idea" is the idea of Good.[4] Though scholars disagree on Plato's view of the divine, it is clear that Plato posits within it the idea of changeless perfection. For anything perfect could only change for the worse. Included in this line of thinking is the idea that emotions produce change, and therefore, that which is perfect may experience no "…joy or sorrow or pleasure."[5]

Also of note, Plato was a primary contributor to the idea of humanity being composed of more than just the physical. According to Ferguson, "…the familiar dichotomy in Western thought between body and soul is a product of the Platonic tradition."[6]

Stoicism and Epicureanism

During the Hellenistic Age, there were two major competing philosophies, both of which drew heavily upon the teachings of Plato: That of the Stoics and that of the Epicureans.[7]

Founded by Zeno of Citium (335-263 BC), the philosophy of stoicism theorized that the ultimate goal in life was achieving *virtue*.[8] Additionally, the Stoics held to a pantheistic view of God.[9] That is, God is found "within and throughout" the world. He is distinct but not separate from natural matter.

While the nearness of God was emphasized in the Stoic worldview, stoicism held to a doctrine of strict determinism.[10] In other words, nothing happens that is not predestined to happen. To that end, I have always been "ordained" to sit here on the beaches of North Carolina as I enjoy my family and take time to pen this book. In the same way, my aunt Pat was predestined to fall unconscious while driving and end up in the hospital on a ventilator and dialysis machine at this very same moment in history. Evil acts can come forth from the will of God because the only truly evil entity is our perspective. Aunt Pat's situation, or even my mother's battle with and ultimate death from alcoholism, will ultimately work together for a greater good.

Lastly, Zeno, like Plato, held that emotion was "an unnatural movement of the mind."[11] Nothing perfect could ever experience something as imperfect as emotion. How can "what is rational" ever experience something so impulsive? This gives much insight into our modern-day perspective on what it means to be a stoic individual.

Stoicism set itself up on the porch (stoa) of public life, while the Epicureans desired a more peaceful and recluse lifestyle. Hedonistic in nature, the philosophy of Epicurus (341-270 BC) theorized that pleasure was the ultimate good and pain the primary evil.

Epicurus was also a materialist. He did not believe in reality outside of the tangible. However, this did not stop him from a belief in gods. He simply suggested that the gods were made of physical matter. Key to our discussion was his idea that the gods never involved themselves with the menial affairs of humans. They were aloof and separate. Petitionary prayer, to Epicurus, was a practice in futility; why would the gods stoop to settling a dispute amongst humanity?

Still, the Epicurean communal way of life is thought to have influenced early Christian fellowships and evidence of the influence of Epicurus' teachings can be found up to New Testament times.[12]

Though I have far too inadequately summarized in a few pages the philosophies of hundreds of years of Hellenistic thinking, I believe the reader can quickly start to pick out some major themes of what it meant to be divine in the years leading up to the birth of Christ:

> **Immutability**: A perfect God could not change, as change would lead to a loss of perfection.

Impassibility: A perfect God could experience no emotion, as emotion indicates change.

Transcendence: The Divine was separate from and uninvolved with humanity. (Of course, the pantheistic-minded Stoics would take some exception here, though they too would lay no claim to the existence of a personal God.)

Determinism: That which Providence determined would happen, would. Humans did not have true free will.

Timelessness: Perfection was not bound by the limitations of time.

And we can trace the transition of Hellenistic thought into New Testament theology, much of which was accomplished through two major historical characters.

Philo (~30 BC-50 AD)

A Jewish scholar with the goal of reconciling Greek thought with biblical teaching, John Sanders calls Philo "…the bridge from the Greeks to the Christians," and "…the leading figure in forging the biblical-classical synthesis."[13] Philo has also been recognized as "…the first to attempt to synthesize revealed faith and philosophic reason."[14, 15]

Brought up through the Greek educational system, Philo would affirm many of the same ideas that formulated the Divine as his Hellenistic predecessors had. To Philo, God was timeless, impassible, and immutable. A student of Scripture, Philo was aware of the many passages that challenged these descriptions, but chose to write them off as anthropomorphisms and not to be taken as literal truths.[16]

Philo's influence cannot be understated. Of particular interest is the influence Philo is thought to have had on the writing of the New Testament, where teachings similar to his appear in John as well as Hebrews. Philo's writings were abundant, including several apologetic writings, many expositions on Pentateuchal Law, and numerous commentaries and interpretations of the Torah. Also of note is the Christian tradition of Philo meeting Peter in Rome and being converted to Christianity.[17]

Augustine (354-430 AD)

Like Philo, Augustine has been recognized as a key player in the merging of the Greek philosophic and Judeo-Christian traditions.[18] Widely quoted and heavily influential, the teachings of this scholar are scarcely found missing from any major Christian theological work of the past century and a half.

Augustine was a student of the teachings of Plotinus,[19] a Neo-Platonist who lived from 204 to 270 AD. The major works of Augustine reflect his inherited Hellenism. In his works the great saint sees God as immutable,[20, 21] impassible,[22] and timeless.[23] Additionally, while both determinists and free will theists can each find something quotable in his body of work to support their viewpoint, Augustine does seem to affirm a deterministic worldview when in his "On Faith, Hope and Love," he states, "But however strong may be the purposes either of angels or of men, whether good or bad… the will of the Omnipotent is never defeated."[24] Augustine is a perfect example of how the beliefs of the scholarly few can persuade and pervade the thinking of the faithful majority.

Affirming a Relational God

The brief history lesson above is not intended as an indictment of early Christian thinking. Nor does Hellenism's influence on modern theological discourse necessarily indicate such an influence resulted in bad theology. In the final analysis, however, the Bible should bear the final answer. If our presuppositions about how a perfect God should look are set aside, the reader will quickly find a compelling case against "traditionalism" in the very texts traditionalists hold so dear.

Immutability

Ascribing immutability to God implies that any change would be a change for the worse, as "how can you alter perfection?" Indeed, the God of the Bible "does not change like the shifting shadows" (James 1:17). Other verses that have been used to defend the immutability stance include:

For I, the LORD, do not change; therefore you, O sons of Jacob, are not consumed. (Mal. 3:6)

God is not a man, that He should lie, Nor a son of man, that He should repent; Has He said, and will He not do it? Or has He spoken, and will He not make it good? (Num. 23:19)

Jesus Christ is the same yesterday and today and forever. (Heb. 13:8)

Google "immutability and God"- Google almost any biblical topic for that matter- and you will find enough "proof texts" to justify any claim about the divine. But as students of Scripture, we should refrain from quoting verses without providing adequate context to their meaning. For example, in stating "Jesus Christ is the same yesterday, today, and forever," was the author of Hebrews truly intending to speak to the immutability of the Godhead, or was he simply encouraging fellow believers by pointing to our God's consistent love and presence in their lives? While an exegetical analysis of each verse in Scripture describing the character of God is far beyond the reach of this book, I would exhort the reader that, as with any serious study of the Bible, the whole counsel of the Word of God should be taken into account before final judgements are made.

Let us take a look at a few passages that would seem to contradict the traditional immutability view:

> **Hezekiah's Illness: In those days Hezekiah became ill and was at the point of death. The prophet Isaiah son of Amoz went to him and said, "This is what the LORD says: Put your house in order, because you are going to die; you will not recover." Hezekiah turned his face to the wall and prayed to the LORD, "Remember, LORD, how I have walked before you faithfully and with wholehearted devotion and have done what is good in your eyes." And Hezekiah wept bitterly. Then the word of the LORD came to Isaiah: "Go and tell Hezekiah, 'This is what the LORD, the God of your father David, says: I have heard your prayer and seen your tears; I will add fifteen years to your life.* (Isa. 38:1-5)

Taken at face value, this passage is a clear example of God's ability to change, specifically, His willingness to change His mind in light of new information. As stated previously, if we wanted to, we could write this type of passage off as anthropomorphism. But why? What else indicates this is required other than our preconceived notions of who God should be? Why not rejoice in the fact that the God of the universe is willing to enter into a give and take relationship with his creation? And, after all, what type of governance requires more sovereignty, one of total control or one of move and countermove? In other words, is it a God who brings about his will through dominance or

One that weaves it through the fabric of man's free choices? Clearly, it is the latter.

A second passage gives a further example of a nimble God:

> ***Nineveh Repents**: Then the word of the LORD came to Jonah a second time: "Go to the great city of Nineveh and proclaim to it the message I give you." Jonah obeyed the word of the LORD and went to Nineveh. Now Nineveh was a very large city; it took three days to go through it. Jonah began by going a day's journey into the city, proclaiming, "Forty more days and Nineveh will be overthrown." The Ninevites believed God. A fast was proclaimed, and all of them, from the greatest to the least, put on sackcloth. When Jonah's warning reached the king of Nineveh, he rose from his throne, took off his royal robes, covered himself with sackcloth and sat down in the dust. This is the proclamation he issued in Nineveh: "By the decree of the king and his nobles: Do not let people or animals, herds or flocks, taste anything; do not let them eat or drink. But let people and animals be covered with sackcloth. Let everyone call urgently on God. Let them give up their evil ways and their violence. Who knows? God may yet relent and with compassion turn from his fierce anger so that we will not perish." When God saw what they did and how they turned from their evil ways, he relented and did not bring on them the destruction he had threatened.* (Jon. 3:1-10)

The traditional, Hellenistic understanding of God also does not allow for this story to be interpreted literally. Not that the reader should mistake God for flippant, as this would be another extreme. The best synthesis of all passages presented in this section is that God is unchanging in who He is but not necessarily in what He does.

Impossibility

The case for changelessness becomes even murkier when we consider the changing emotions of God. Several verses illustrate that God is intimately responsive to the actions of man.

> *They built high places for Baal in the Valley of Ben Hinnom to sacrifice their sons and daughters to Molek, though I never commanded—nor did it enter my mind—that they should do such a detestable thing and so make Judah sin.* (Jer. 32:35)

The passage has far-reaching implications in relation to God's foreknowledge as well. Specifically here, though, this passage indicates divine surprise.

> *How can I give you up, Ephraim? How can I hand you over, Israel? How can I treat you like Admah? How can I make you like Zeboyim? My heart is changed within me; all my compassion is aroused.* (Hos. 11:8)

Similarly:

> *The LORD regretted that he had made human beings on the earth, and his heart was deeply troubled.* (Gen. 6:6)

In this last verse, God is reacting to the evil acts humans have committed since their creation. Many more passages may be cited, but I will let these examples stand as evidence that, when read without presupposition, that the Bible describes an emotion-filled, interactive God.

As to the topics of timelessness vs. temporality and determinism vs. free will, these will be dealt with in more detail in later chapters.

Existential Implications-Why does it matter?

As we close out the first chapter, I would like to take a few lines to make sure we are keeping this discussion in perspective. Why even raise such critiques? Shouldn't we worry less about parsing polysyllabic words and more about "love" and "reaching the lost?" As evangelicals, of course these are the primary concerns. Let us not fail in our desire, however, to introduce our Creator accurately. A relational, loving God is far more appealing to a world in need than a stoic deity. We are charged with being a light to a dying world. When the lampshade of traditionalism is removed, the light shines much brighter!

CHAPTER 2

How God Ordained Free Choice

In the last chapter, I attempted to demonstrate the influence Greek thought had on the modern evangelical view of God. This chapter serves as an extension of that theme, with a specific focus on one divine attribute ascribed to the governance of the gods of Hellenism: *determinism*.

No doubt a God that predestines all things is appealing for several reasons. It is certainly a comforting thought to be assured that nothing happens outside of God's foreordained plan. Corollary to that line of thinking is that we are ultimately not responsible for the decisions that we make. Certainly, as an evangelical, there is much less pressure in seeing that a lost world comes to a saving faith. For those that "refuse to choose" were never truly meant for the Kingdom of Heaven in the first place.

But theorizing such a God also brings with it some troubling thoughts. If God predestines all things, then what about the occurrence of evil? If evil in general seems non-problematic to the reader, what happens when we discuss specifics? Surely the foreordination of millions of Jews dying at the hands of sadistic Nazi experimentation is less palatable to the reader. Evil aside, what of natural disaster? What about eternal damnation for the non-believer? The stoic god of determinism may seem appealing at first, but is this the God of the Bible? What's more, is this the God we want to present to the faithless?

This chapter will introduce *determinism* as a system of theology and then attempt to respond to what is still a majority view amongst most evangelical theologians. I will then address some of the major reasons traditionalists often reject free will theologies.

History of the Calvinist-Arminian Controversy

*From this point on in the chapter, I will refer to the *Church* in italics when referring to the *Church* as the "body of believers" at large, in order to differentiate references to the Roman Catholic Church.

Doctrinal division has existed in the *Church* from its very beginning. In Galatians Chapter 2, for instance, we read of Paul opposing Peter because of Peter's concern that it may be inappropriate to eat with the Gentiles.[1] Years later, the Council of Nicaea assembles and refutes Arius's famous claim that Christ was not fully man and fully divine.[2] Shortly thereafter we see Augustine refuting Pelagius and his rejection of the doctrine of Original Sin.[3] Perhaps no doctrinal disagreements stand more prominent in history than that which led to the Protestant Reformation and the division of the Roman Catholic Church.

In the last chapter, we spoke of the influence Augustine had on the *Church's* theology. One of the more controversial views he held was his belief that salvation could only be obtained through the vehicle of the Catholic Church.[4] The outplaying of this concept resulted in great institutional and political power for the Roman Catholics. As Mildred Bangs Wynkoop states, "This [belief helped lead to] the… unbiblical and sometimes immoral abuses of the system of 'indulgences' which tied the individual to the Church… heart and purse… and encouraged him in his sins."[5] The *indulgences* promoted by the Catholic Church were a way of selling forgiveness of sins: A parishioner can be made right with God through paying a penalty to the Church. It is plain to see, if the Church holds the power of salvation, how such a system could be easily mishandled.

Both Martin Luther (1483-1546) and John Calvin (1509-1564) stood up to these abuses as the great reformers of their time, beginning a period in *Church* history aptly known as "The Reformation." In order to oppose the Catholic doctrine of salvation through the Church, Calvin placed a large emphasis on the role God plays in the salvation of man. He taught that it was not the Church but God who decides if a man is to be "saved." Also borrowing from Augustine (interestingly enough), he preached a strict *determinism*. That is, God "elects" some men for salvation and some for damnation. (A student of Calvin, Theodore Beza, would later take Calvin's teaching to the logical conclusion that it was God who causes man to sin.[6])

As Calvin's teachings became the predominant theology of the Reformation, Dutch layman Dirik Koornheert began to openly oppose them. He caused such a public stir that James Arminius (1560-1609), an educated disciple of Calvin, was commissioned to refute Koornheert's opposition. Ironically, Arminius' research brought him to also break from Calvin's doctrinal views.

The followers of Arminius (known as the "Remonstrants") and those of Calvin would go on in a public hearing, known as the Synod of Dort, in 1618 to summarize their respective theologies as described on the following page.[7]

Five Points of the Remonstrants	**Five Points of Calvinism**
Conditional Election	**Unconditional Election**
God predestines man for salvation on the basis of the foreknowledge of who will choose Him.	Salvation is the choice of God, not the free choice of man.
Universal Atonement	**Limited Atonement**
Christ died for all sinners.	Christ's death was only an atonement for the elect.
Natural Inability	**Total Depravity**
Man cannot do good apart from the grace of God.	Man must be sparked to change before he can be saved.
Prevenient Grace	**Irresistible Grace**
Grace allows mankind to do good and turn to God.	Grace is only given to the elect, and cannot be rejected.
Conditional Perseverance	**Perseverance of the Saints**
Once saved, salvation can be forfeited.	Once saved, salvation cannot be forfeited.

"Determining" What is Right

So why another history lesson? Ultimately, it is of utmost importance to know the history of how a doctrine comes about. A theology built solely on the proper exposition of Scripture should hold more value to the reader than one based on reactionism. As history indicates, "The theory of personal predestination was not... derived from biblical exegesis but was a doctrine demanded by logical necessity to defend the absolute sovereignty of God against the sovereignty of the Church.[8]"

But clearly, the origin of the view does not necessarily negate its validity. So what evidence is there in support of the determinism world view?

The Case for Determinism

The primary argument for determinism is not so much that it can be supported biblically, but that any other view would undermine the sovereignty of God. Committed Calvinist R. C. Sproul puts it this way:

> The movement of every molecule, the actions of every planet, the falling of every star, the choices of every volitional creature, all of these are subject to His sovereign will. No maverick molecules run loose in the universe... if such a molecule existed, it could be the critical fly in the eternal ointment.[9]

In other words, if God is not in control of all things, then He is not perfect. He is weak and vulnerable to the unpredictability of His creation. By logical necessity, the deterministic worldview must be reality, since it is the only worldview that maintains an adequate perception of the Creator.

Of course, Christian determinists cite Scripture to support their theology. Isaiah 46:8-11 seems to state the case clearly:

> *Remember this, keep it in mind, take it to heart, you rebels. Remember the former things, those of long ago; I am God, and there is no other; I am God, and there is none like me. I make known the end from the beginning, from ancient times, what is still to come. I say, 'My purpose will stand, and I will do all that I please.' From the east I summon a bird of prey from a far-off land, a man to fulfill my purpose. What I have said, that I will bring about; what I have planned, that I will do.*

Phrases such as "my purpose will stand," and "what I have planned, that I will do," clearly implicate God as the master manipulator, right?

Perhaps no passage in Scripture has been used more frequently to defend the determinist's position than Romans Chapter 9: 11-24:

Yet, before the twins were born or had done anything good or bad—in order that God's purpose in election might stand: not by works but by him who calls—she was told, "The older will serve the younger." Just as it is written: "Jacob I loved, but Esau I hated."

What then shall we say? Is God unjust? Not at all! For he says to Moses, "I will have mercy on whom I have mercy, and I will have compassion on whom I have compassion."

It does not, therefore, depend on human desire or effort, but on God's mercy. For Scripture says to Pharaoh: "I raised you up for this very purpose, that I might display my power in you and that my name might be proclaimed in all the earth." Therefore God has mercy on whom he wants to have mercy, and he hardens whom he wants to harden. One of you will say to me: "Then why does God still blame us? For who is able to resist his will?" But who are you, a human being, to talk back to God? "Shall what is formed say to the one who formed it, 'Why did you make me like this?'" Does not the potter have the right to make out of the same lump of clay some pottery for special purposes and some for common use?

What if God, although choosing to show his wrath and make his power known, bore with great patience the objects of his wrath—prepared for destruction? What if he did this to make the riches of his glory known to the objects of his mercy, whom he prepared in advance for glory—even us, whom he also called, not only from the Jews but also from the Gentiles?

Combine the views of some of the most influential thinkers in world history with a text like this and how could you not walk away a determinist?! Clearly, God chooses who He wants to have mercy on and prepares others for destruction. So compelling is this passage that it is the exact one that James Arminius went to in order to defend the *Church* from the assumedly errant views of Koornheert.

But we also know that Arminius walked away from his research as an opponent of the deterministic world view. So what did he find that could help shed light on the meaning of this passage?

An Answer to the Calvinist View of Romans Chapter 9

Read as a whole, the major theme of the book of Romans is "the power of God in salvation." When viewed in context, Paul is speaking in Chapter 9 to the Jews' rejection of Christ as Savior and God's willingness to use the Gentiles as a vehicle to bring them back to the Truth. As such, Romans 9 affirms the election of the saints, but on a corporate (versus a personal) scale. In other words, in God's sovereignty, He chose the Gentiles to be incorporated into the "vine" of God's mercy. Whereas in the past, salvation had only come through belonging to the nation of Israel.

What of the example Paul uses when speaking of Jacob and Esau? These details seem very personal, but is a reference to personal predestination what the readers of Paul's epistle would have understood? I would argue not. To Jacob belonged the birthright of the nation of Israel; to Esau, the birthright of a rebellious nation.[10] This is what first century Jews would have heard loud and clear in Paul's exposition: God is choosing the Gentiles now, just as He chose the nation of Israel millennia ago. The Jews should not object to His choice, since it is just. "I will have mercy on whom I will have mercy. And compassion on whom I will have compassion." Further, if the reader will venture to Romans 9:25-33, she will see the theme of national election bared in Paul's conclusions.

Biblical Argument for Free Choice

Any passage rightly studied should be taken in the context of the full revelation of Scripture. There is an abundance of passages that affirm the role that man must play, not only in the salvific process but in the course of his daily life.

> *And if it is evil in your eyes to serve the Lord, choose this day whom you will serve, whether the gods your fathers served in the region beyond the River, or the gods of the Amorites in whose land you dwell.* (Josh. 24:15)

> *Behold, I stand at the door and knock. If anyone hears my voice and opens the door, I will come in to him and eat with him, and he with me.* (Rev. 3:20)

> *I call heaven and earth to witness against you today, that I have set before you life and death, blessing and curse. Therefore choose life, that you and your offspring may live, loving the Lord your God, obeying his voice and holding fast to him...* (Deut. 30:19-20)

This chapter could be filled with verses implying free will, but I'm afraid it would begin to feel redundant. So we are left with a choice (no pun intended): either the Bible is not genuine when speaking of the choices we must make or there is some secret agenda that God doesn't want the reader to know about. I would argue the former over the latter. God is not someone who handpicks a chosen few for salvation, rather He is a God who "desires all people to be saved and to come to the knowledge of the truth."[11]

Foreknowledge and Freedom

I argue that the primary reason the deterministic worldview has taken such a stronghold in the minds of modern theologians is that the arguments in opposition have been weak at best.

Traditional *free will theists* have reconciled passages which may imply determinism within their system of theology by simply stating God looks into the future to see what man will do and predestines them according to that knowledge. Romans 8:29 seems to exemplify this viewpoint:

For those God foreknew he also predestined to be conformed to the image of his Son, that he might be the firstborn among many brothers and sisters.

At first, this may seem to the reader a reasonable solution to the problems presented by strict determinists. But does God foreknowing the future and predestining man for salvation (or any act for that matter) based on that knowledge really provide an adequate medium in which free will may play out? I think the silence of the lack of scholarship defending that stance is answer enough.

I'll illustrate the objectionableness of traditional incompatibilism with an example used by theologian William Hasker in his book "God, Time and Knowledge." In the following scenario, Clarence, an expert omelet maker, is going to have a cheese omelet for breakfast tomorrow. Assuming God foreknows this event will occur, the logic-based argument that Clarence will not make a free will choice in deciding to make the omelet goes as follows:

(1) It is true that Clarence will have a cheese omelet for breakfast tomorrow. (Premise)

(2) It is impossible that God should at any time believe what is false, or fail to believe anything that is true. (Premise: divine omniscience)

(3) Therefore, God has always believed that Clarence will have a cheese omelet for breakfast tomorrow. (From 1, 2)

(4) If God has always believed a certain thing, it is not in anyone's power to bring it about that God has not always believed that thing. (Premise: the unalterability of the past)

(5) Therefore, it is not in Clarence's power to bring it about that God has not already believed that he would have a cheese omelet for breakfast. (From 3,4)

(6) It is not possible for it to be true both that God has always believed that Clarence would have a cheese omelet for breakfast, and that he does not in fact have one. (From 2)

(7) Therefore, it is not in Clarence's power to refrain from having a cheese omelet for breakfast tomorrow (From 5,6) So Clarence's eating the omelet tomorrow is not an act of free will.[12]

The validity of this argument if furthered by the fact that professor and Arminian theologian Jon Tal Murphree argues that, if God does possess direct foreknowledge of the future, He may choose not to access the information.[13] (For if He did access it, no choice would truly be free.) The argument is respectable, but Dr. Murphree is unfortunately willing to compromise sound reason for the sake of traditionalism.

Perhaps the most compelling reason traditional incompatibilism does not see much support in scholarship is its lack of existential application. In other words, let's assume free will can exist in a world in which God foreknows the future. To what use could that foreknowledge be put? Again, let me illustrate with an example. This example involves an avid cyclist—Steve—making a catastrophic error in judgment:

> *Steve had a late night last night. A newborn child, a sick wife, and the planning of his best friend's upcoming bachelor party were more than the right prescription for his current groggy state of mind. Late to work, Steve was pedaling much more quickly than usual. As he approached a railroad track that he had never actually seen a train on, he decided to continue "full steam ahead" without bothering to stop. Steve didn't notice the rumbling of the oncoming train, and he hit the tracks just in time to meet his untimely end.*

A morbid scenario, sure. Isn't it such an extreme situation that we would like God to put His foreknowledge to use? The reader might state if God foreknew yesterday this event would occur today, then He could intervene and make sure Steve gets a good night of sleep so his judgment would not be altered. Simpler yet, maybe He could just divinely alert Steve to the oncoming train. By holding to the traditional foreknowledge view, we would only have two options:

1. God's foreknowledge of Steve's death is accurate, and Steve dies in the train crash.

2. God makes sure Steve gets to work safely, *in which case God could not have foreknown Steve was going to die in the first place*.

It should not be hard for an Arminian reader to let go of his viewpoint that God can directly foresee the future. For if he can, knowledge gained by such foresight is necessarily useless.

No Time, No Problem

Of course, it may seem logical for God to have an exhaustive knowledge of future events simply because such a view is necessitated by the belief that God exists outside of time. He is in the future, so He must know what the future entails. But is God's timelessness a biblically ascribed attribute, or is it a characteristic derived from Hellenism and adopted by early Christian thinkers? I argue the latter option is more compelling. There is no verse in Scripture that necessitates God existing timelessly, and the view creates yet another intellectual barrier for the non-believer to sign up for the Christian faith. "What does it mean to exist outside of time?" he might ask. "How is that even possible if time is simply a reference point of activity?" Or even, "If God simultaneously exists in the past, present, and future, is Jesus being crucified as we speak?" Clearly, the most compelling presentation of the God of the Bible must forego ties to the thinking of the past.

Existential Implications—Why does it matter?

So how can we biblically portray God? The deterministic God of Calvinist theology is not adequate. Though Calvinism was built upon good intentions, the God of the Bible is one who created man with the ability to freely choose Him and enter into a meaningful, loving relationship. Also inadequate are some of the traditional responses given in defense of free will theology. A God who foreknows is logically a God who determines, and the concept of a timeless being is unintelligible.

Why not let the Bible speak for itself? We must present to the unbeliever a God of love, of relationship, and of intimate, timely, and genuine interaction. The boundaries created by traditional theology do not allow for this. Perhaps this is made no clearer than when discussing the problem of pain. And to that we now turn.

CHAPTER 3

The Problem of the Problem of Pain

> To ask if the universe as we see it looks more like the work of a wise and good Creator, or the work of chance... is to omit from the outset... the relevant factors in the religious problem. Christianity is not the conclusion of a philosophical debate... it is a catastrophic historical event... it is not a system into which we have to fit the awkward fact of pain; it is itself one of the awkward facts which has to be fitted into any system we make... It creates rather than solves the problem of pain, for pain would be no problem unless... we had received... a good assurance that ultimate reality is righteous and loving.
>
> —C.S. Lewis in "The Problem of Pain"[1]

I have read no better definition given to "the problem of pain" than the preceding quote. In his remarks, Lewis draws attention to the fact that the existence of suffering within humanity is only problematic because of humanity's ultimate belief that there exists a "righteous and loving" Creator who oversees our affairs. In other words, if only chaos governed the universe, what expectation of goodness could we ultimately have? This unease that exists in the world is a good thing: it shows that the non-believer, if only subconsciously, is searching for a way to reconcile belief in a power higher than himself.

But have Christians done an adequate job in providing an acceptable answer to "the problem of pain"? Or do the quips and pat answers often provided in the face of suffering do more harm than good? What follows is an example of extreme turmoil. Hopefully the response Trudy receives from her pastor in light of her suffering will serve to exemplify the issue we have created out of "the problem of pain":

Trudy was a faithful Christian. Committing her life to Christ over twenty years ago, she had experienced her spiritual "ups and downs," but there was always a way to find the grace of God in every situation. Perhaps the greatest trial of her life was her three-year battle with lymphoma. Yet, even in her darkest valleys, God's love showed true. Though her treatment bankrupted them, her husband Tony had stuck by her side the whole way. By a miracle, two years later, Trudy was even able to conceive the child she was told she would never be able to have. Five years in remission, financially and emotionally back on their feet, life was good for the Jones household. That was true, at least, until last November.

At 8:30pm November 12th, 2014, Trudy got the phone call no wife and mother ever wants to receive. Tony, driving home from Trudy's spontaneously requested fast food run, got side-swiped by a drunk driver. Sent careening into a ravine, the car flipped three times before it came to a stop over a hundred feet below the road. Five-year-old Steven had been in the back seat, opting at the last minute to tag along with dad. Both Tony and Steven were pronounced dead on the scene.

Now eight months later, Trudy was still an emotional wreck. The questions she had asked from the minute she heard the news still ran unanswered through her mind. Why me? How, after all that we've been through, could my dreams come to an end so mercilessly? Why would God allow such a terrible thing to happen? And that was perhaps the most disturbing thing. Her God, who had been her fortress and strength for the past twenty-five years, seemed so distant. Trudy had always believed that everything happened for a reason. But try as she may, she couldn't discern why God would allow the two people she loved the most to be stolen from her hands.

Her pastor, a family friend of over fifty years, did his best to console Trudy. As he prayed and cried with her, Trudy tried her best to take comfort in his words. "Sometimes we can't see it, but there is a greater good behind everything that happens. God would not let this occur if He didn't think you were strong enough to handle it." For all she had already been through, though, Trudy somehow didn't feel that strong.

Finding Comfort in Determinism

Consistent with what's been argued previously, the traditional view of why "bad things happen to good people" lies in Hellenistic roots. According to the Stoic view of the divine, "nothing happens that was not providentially ordained by God."[2] Augustine follows suit with his philosophic predecessors, refusing to deviate in even the most extreme of circumstances. When speaking of infant death, Augustine opines, "Perhaps God is doing some good in correcting parents when their beloved children suffer pain and even death."[3]

To presuppose God's hand in causing tragedy may seem extreme to many, but this line of thinking permeates the counsel of Christians, lay and pastoral alike. Gregory Boyd, in his book, "Is God to Blame?" calls this the *Blueprint Worldview*[4]*:* the idea that everything that happens to us occurs for a reason and, though the explanation may not be clear at the time, God has a plan behind every wrong that occurs. I prefer to call this mindset *Greater Good Theology*, since the verse most often used to support it is Romans 8:28, which states *"And we know that in all things God works for the good of those who love him, who have been called according to his purpose."*

Perhaps the most commonly misused verse in Scripture, it can frequently be found on the lips of the Christian comforter as a citation of proof that there is a "greater good" behind every evil that has ever and will ever occur. Is that really what Paul is saying here in his epistle? Moreover, is this what we want it to say?

The implications of such a claim are what make *Greater Good Theology* so unpalatable to so many. For on the one who makes the claims that all of mankind's ills are foreordained for the purpose of bringing about a great good lies the burden of divining a reason for some of the greatest tragedies of history. The 11 million Jewish and non-Jewish deaths that occurred during the holocaust, the 60+ million deaths during WWII, even the 3,000 Americans deaths on 9/11 come to mind as just a few examples that may give the *Greater Good* theologian pause.

Examples aren't just found on the macro level. What of significant personal tragedy? Though the pastor in my fabricated story tries, it is very hard to look someone in the eyes who has suffered something so catastrophic as the loss of spouse and child and tell them God took away her dearest loved ones out of pursuit of a better plan. It's not hard to see why Trudy may not have found this suggestion very comforting.

What's even more interesting is that *Greater Good Theology* seems to be a mainstay of the evangelical church, even for those who would claim to favor free will over determinism. This will be discussed more deeply in a later chapter, but it seems that Hellenistic thinking so permeates Christianity that even those who intellectually oppose the predestination worldview have a pseudo-deterministic default when it comes to the problem of pain. How many of us, when going through a difficult time, have been offered the consolation in the form of "God is in control" or "God has a better plan"? Who among us can say they find assigning the blame of tragedy to a good God truly comforting?

The Culpability of Allowing

Traditional Arminianism tries to solve the difficulties raised by the deterministic solution to the "problem of pain". James 1:13 states, "God cannot be tempted by evil, nor does he tempt anyone. But each person is tempted when they are dragged away by their own evil desire and enticed." Jesus' earthly brother James is clearly implying here that God is not the author of evil acts. Was the extinction of the Jewish race an achievement God tempted Hitler towards, or was Hitler simply led on the path down which his corrupt desires for fame and power led him? James would choose the latter option. The same can be said for the more recent shooting of nine innocent black church goers in Charleston, South Carolina, by a white supremacist.

To the Arminian, God does not foreordain evil. However, if God is a God who has an exhaustive foreknowledge of the future (as Arminians claim), why doesn't He take steps to stop such calamities? (I have already argued previously that foreknowledge equates to determinism and that simple foreknowledge is useless. Let's even set those two points aside.) The Arminian answer is that God "allows" evil to occur. Clearly, though, evil doesn't *always* occur at times when it could. More clearly still, good doesn't *always* prevail against injustice. So if God simply "allows" evils to occur, He must be picking and choosing between them. How does this not assess culpability to God?! The fact of the matter is that every traditional answer to the "problem of pain" ends in assigning God ultimate responsibility.

God looks like Jesus

In our hearts, we know this can't be. Only a mind jaded by years of the study of theology and not the Bible, colluding with cronies and not the Creator, could ever reach an ultimate conclusion that puts *any* blame for evil on a loving, just God. But if God does not determine evil and also does not "allow" evil, then how do we explain its occurrence? I think the challenge can be met by looking at the best presentation of God's providence that He ever gave us: the life of God made flesh, Jesus.

There are several passages throughout the gospels in which Jesus is confronted with evil and its resulting pain. We can look at the time where Jesus confronts the money-changers at the temple,[5] or the death of Lazarus,[6] or even the Great Injustice of His death on the cross.[7] As God on earth, Jesus was a man who fought against injustice, wept over tragedy, and sought to comfort rather than reason during times of deep loss. There was never a time when Jesus espoused the philosophy of determinism. He didn't explain away the existence of the infirm and impoverished using Greater Good theology. Yes, He came as a servant to serve,[8] but also as a crusader, inspiring others to the fight.

Jesus' mission on Earth was "to proclaim good news to the poor... to proclaim freedom for the prisoners and recovery of sight for the blind, to set the oppressed free."[9] Jesus never caused oppression. He never imprisoned anyone in sickness or poverty so they might learn a greater lesson. Jesus was the Ultimate Fighter, a champion of those who suffered, who wanted nothing for them but to bring them into His loving Kingdom.

If this is the portrayal of God on earth, why should we expect our Father in Heaven to act differently? Yes, we know in order for freedom to exist, evil must as well. By definition, true "free will" must allow for the ability for free agents to reject goodness. In a fallen creation, sickness and natural disasters coexist with peace and tranquility. In such a world, suffering and pain are an inevitable. For God's great experiment of creation to be meaningful, this is how it had to be. That by no means implies God *ever wants* His beloved- those created in His image- to suffer and experience pain.

During a time of trial and tragedy, this is the God I want to experience: One who weeps with me and is there to comfort. Not only that, one who has experienced suffering

Himself and has the power to bring me through so that I am a better person and closer to Him because of it. The last thing I want to do is be counseled regarding a mysterious and aloof Being who has an ultimate plan for why He either "caused" or "allowed" my spouse and child to die in a car accident, bones crushed under tons of steel, as their way too short of lives flashed before them. Traditional evangelicalism will continue to provide an inadequate place of refuge for the hopeless and hurting of the world as long as we let the traditions of the Church place a roadblock in front of the comfort of the Creator.

Offering Genuine Comfort

So then what should we say to Trudy in her time of greatest hurt? Maybe nothing. Maybe she would find greater solace in simply having a shoulder to cry on. Perhaps, as cliché as it may sound, we should ask ourselves, "What would Jesus do?" If we take this simple step, we may quickly realize that, in times of intense sorrow, love trumps logic, tears surpass traditions, and the promise of hope triumphs over the pain inflicted by pat answers.

Choosing to share His eternal, Trinitarian love with others, God chose to enter into a cosmic struggle with evil in order to draw His creation into eternal communion. Somehow, thousands of years after the struggle began, we have lost sight of the simplicity of love in favor of our systems of theology. The Trudys of the world suffer because of it. Maybe Trudy would not feel so distant from God if she realized *God never wants evil and always wants good.* The problem with the problem of pain is that the Church has unwittingly assigned blame for the pain on the One who most deeply wishes it would cease. Knowing that the Omnipotent One is by her side during her time of loss is what would give Trudy the strength to move past her pain.

Nothing less will do.

Let us, as Christ followers, portray *that* God, the God of Comfort, to a hurting world, lifting Him up for who He is not our preconceived notions of who we want Him to be. If we accomplish that simple task, we have His promise that we will watch in joy as all are drawn unto Him.[10]

CHAPTER 4

Is Eternal Suffering for the Masses?

> God has been made so cruel, and this doctrine is so unthinkable that it has probably created more atheists, and caused more weak believers to fall away than any other false teaching. The dread of Hell has caused misery and mental anguish to countless millions and instead of the horror of hell turning many to God... many millions have been turned away from such an unjust God.
>
> —William West, "The Resurrection and Immortality"

> How can Christians possibly portray a deity of such cruelty and vindictiveness whose ways include inflicting everlasting torture upon His creatures, however sinful they may have been?
>
> —Clark Pinnock, "The Destruction of the Finally Impenitent"

The Philosophy of Eternal Suffering

Abrasive words aren't spared from those who disagree with the traditional doctrine of eternal torment of nonbelievers in hell. Though I side with the above criticisms, I have refrained from quoting even harsher verbiage. Certainly, the debate over the doctrine of hell evokes passion from all sides. Why? What exactly is at stake as theologians verbally spar over what, on its face, seems like just one more topic regarding which the Bible doesn't provide definitive clarity?

Speaking as one who affirms the doctrine of "conditional immortality" (or that those who die without a saving faith in Christ cease to exist rather than suffer eternal, conscious torment), I see much at stake. First and foremost, the belief that our Heavenly Father would sentence any man to an eternity of conscious pain and anguish *for any reason* calls into question the very character of God. Few evangelicals would disagree that the God of the Bible is one of love.[1] How can it be loving, though, to send a temporal being to an eternal torture chamber? The reader might argue that God is equally just as He is loving, and this may allow her to reason for the legitimacy of the traditional view of hell. But while receiving justice for our sins might very well result in separation from God,[2] nowhere in the Bible does it necessitate conscious suffering.

Secondly, most honest scholars will concede the Bible is at best unclear on the mode of eternal punishment for the non-believer. So why should we default to the least attractive view? Perhaps there was a time in the Church's history when the sinner could be scared into a saving faith. Who can forget Jonathan Edwards' famous 18th century sermon *Sinners in the Hands of an Angry God*? In a postmodern era, however, in which skepticism and intellectualism reign supreme, very few people are frightened by the tired vision of a devil, a pitchfork, and a burning pit. Most, to the contrary, are rather turned off by it. This can be seen by the lack of affinity passersby have towards the occasional fire and brimstone preacher on a street corner. If the threat of eternal torment was a successful means of delivering the Good News to the lost, one would think more people would be interested in his message.

But this is not the case. Most thoughtful people in our culture today are rather turned off by the concept of what they see as such an unscrupulous god. Pastor and author Gregory Boyd published a series of dialogues that he and his father had about the Christian faith in his book *Letters from a Skeptic*. In this publication, Boyd converses with his atheist father in hopes of winning him to a saving faith in God. As the book came to an end, the last major issue Boyd's father could not overcome was the contradiction he found between a loving God and the punishment of eternal suffering. A glimpse of this letter will be illustrative:

> *Your last letter put my mind a bit more at ease about who is going to hell, but it didn't address the problem of hell itself. This is really the more fundamental question… Now tell me, what the hell (excuse the pun) would be the purpose of torturing someone eternally? What's the point? Obviously there's no "lesson" to be learned… So it just doesn't make sense to me Greg.*

And I'm just not at the point where I can "suspend" judgment about this. The character of god is on trial in my life, and this is very relevant evidence which needs to be considered.

—Gregory Boyd Sr. in Gregory Boyd's "Letters from a Skeptic"

I hope I am not spoiling the end of a good read to say that, after presented with the logic of the view of conditional immortality Mr. Boyd ceases to find the doctrine of hell a barrier to faith and submits his life to the loving God of the Bible. What follows in this chapter is a scriptural argument for the conditional mortality, or annihilationist view of Hell. I would ask the reader to approach the topic with prayerful consideration as, like no other traditional doctrine of God, the implications of blindly holding to such a belief as the eternal conscious suffering of the non-believer are staggering at a minimum.

Origin of the Traditional View

So if conditional immortality is to be argued, what must first be addressed is the question of how the Church could have possibly gotten it so wrong. As in the previous chapters, the answer lies in the teachings of Hellenism, which were contemporary to the formation of Christian thought. Unlike above, the major influence here is the thinking that the soul is naturally immortal. Plato clearly taught so. In fact, he is a primary source cited when philosophers argue the indestructibility of the soul. In his dialogue *Phaedo,* Plato presents his teacher, Socrates, encouraging the reader that there is nothing to fear in death and that the soul eternally continues on. He provides four separate arguments in support of this view (known as the Argument from Opposites, the Theory of Recollection, the Argument from Affinity, and the Argument based on Forms).[3]

Augustine, following the philosophic heritage of Plotinus and Plato, also formed an argument from intellectualism for the immortality of the soul in his writing *The City of God.*[4] This was also a belief John Calvin would adopt.[5] With the opinion that the soul is by nature immortal comes the necessary conclusion that it can never be destroyed. In other words, if one dies and is not destined to spend the remainder of eternity with God in Heaven, there must be a place for that soul to reside.

But is the doctrine of the soul's immortality supported in Scripture? An honest review of popular passages would compel us to conclude not.

On the Natural Mortality of the Soul

Beginning in the book of Genesis, conditional immortality is taught. Among the punishments Adam and Eve received for their transgressions against God was the removal of the chance of an everlasting existence. *"And the LORD God said, 'The man has now become like one of us, knowing good and evil. He must not be allowed to reach out his hand and take also from the tree of life and eat, and live forever.⁶'"* Immortality was a gift and, at least in their current state of sin, the option of achieving it was taken away from our most ancient ancestors.

In fact, the threat of ultimate destruction permeates the Scriptures. Just a handful of verses giving reference to the fact include:

> *****Matthew 10:28**-Do not be afraid of those who kill the body but cannot kill the soul. Rather, be afraid of the One who can destroy both soul and body in hell.*
>
> *****James 4:12**-There is only one Lawgiver and Judge, the one who is able to save and destroy.*
>
> *****2 Thessalonians 1:8-9**-He will punish those who do not know God and do not obey the gospel of our Lord Jesus. They will be punished with everlasting destruction and shut out from the presence of the Lord and from the glory of his might...*
>
> *****Philippians 3:18-19a**-For, as I have often told you before and now tell you again even with tears, many live as enemies of the cross of Christ. Their destiny is destruction...*

Taken on its face, the Bible clearly seems to be warning the sinner that the ultimate price of his transgressions is destruction, not torment. There is no other natural reading of the above passages. It is at best intellectually dishonest to try to interpret "everlasting destruction" as continued conscious existence. Plato added much to philosophic discourse, but the authors of Scripture would take issue with his views on the afterlife.

On the contrary to traditional thinking, the Bible offers immortality to only those who uphold the Good News. 2 Timothy 1:9b-10 states, "*This grace was given us in Christ Jesus before the beginning of time, but it has now been revealed through the appearing of our Savior, Christ Jesus, who has destroyed death and has brought life and immortality to light through the gospel.*" If the Gospel holds the key to immortality, it is logical to assume the rejection of that same Gospel brings the punishment of death.

The doctrine of conditional immortality is given further support through how Jesus described hell in the Gospels. When He referred to the punishment of the sinner, He used the word Gehenna, which has since been directly translated as "hell". Gehenna was a garbage dump outside the city of Jerusalem. At the dump, the fire constantly burned, and whatever was thrown into it was immediately incinerated. So in Matthew 10:28 (see above) when Jesus said the body and soul of the unbeliever would be destroyed in "Gehenna" (or "hell"), His listeners would immediately relate the referenced punishment to the process of consumption by fire.

Problem Passages

So if the teachings of Jesus regarding hell imply conditional immortality and if several other passages support that view, where do opponents of the doctrine find their biblical support? Let's look at a couple of passages traditionalists use.

> ***Isaiah 66:24**- And they will go out and look on the dead bodies of those who rebelled against me; the worms that eat them will not die, the fire that burns them will not be quenched, and they will be loathsome to all mankind.*

Advocates of the eternal torment view point out the worm that inflicts the suffering "will not die." Further, "the fire… will not be quenched." Does this not indicate eternal hellfire? Maybe. It says nothing about eternal consciousness for the non-believer. Look back at Jesus' Gehenna reference. The fires never went out at the dump, but clearly the trash thrown in was destroyed. What's more, the writer of Isaiah provides his own clarity. The first part of the verse states, "And they will go out and look on the dead bodies of those who rebelled against me." Rather than a verse that supports the traditional view of hell, Isaiah 66:24 speaks against it. If the bodies of the condemned are dead, how could they possibly be suffering?

> **Revelation 14:11-***And the smoke of their torment will rise for ever and ever. There will be no rest day or*

> *night for those who worship the beast and its image, or for anyone who receives the mark of its name.*

On its face, this passage may seem slightly more troubling for the annihilationist. A closer look will ease the mind, as the only endless event described here is the ascending "smoke of [the] torment" of the lost soul. Surely its presence will be a sign to the believer of the righteous judgment of God, but this in no way indicates the objects of His punishment will be writhing in pain underneath. That there will be no rest for those who receive the mark of the beast cannot be a reflection of the eternal state as what need is there for day or night in eternity (Rev. 22:5)?

> **Revelation 20:10**-*And they marched up over the broad plain of the earth and surrounded the camp of the saints and the beloved city, but fire came down from heaven and consumed them, and the devil who had deceived them was thrown into the lake of fire and sulfur where the beast and the false prophet were, and they will be tormented day and night forever and ever.*

This is the only passage in the whole of Scripture that clearly speaks to eternal conscious suffering. It must be noted that the only ones receiving such an extreme punishment make up the unholy trinity.

Luke 16:19-31-*There was a rich man who was dressed in purple and fine linen and lived in luxury every day. At his gate was laid a beggar named Lazarus, covered with sores and longing to eat what fell from the rich man's table. Even the dogs came and licked his sores. The time came when the beggar died and the angels carried him to Abraham's side. The rich man also died and was buried. In Hades, where he was in torment, he looked up and saw Abraham far away, with Lazarus by his side. So he called to him, "Father Abraham, have pity on me and send Lazarus to dip the tip of his finger in water and cool my tongue, because I am in agony in this fire."*

But Abraham replied, "Son, remember that in your lifetime you received your good things, while Lazarus received bad things, but now he is comforted here and you are in agony. And besides all this, between us and you a great chasm has been set in place, so that those who want to go from here to you cannot, nor can anyone cross over from there to us.

He answered, "Then I beg you, father, send Lazarus to my family, for I have five brothers. Let him warn them, so that they will not also come to this place of torment."

Abraham replied, "They have Moses and the Prophets; let them listen to them." "No, father Abraham," he said, "but if someone from the dead goes to them, they will repent."

> *He said to him, "If they do not listen to Moses and the Prophets, they will not be convinced even if someone rises from the dead."*

The story of the *Rich Man and Lazarus* is frequently cited as a defense against conditional immortality. If the rich man is suffering in hell, then this parable provides proof positive of the eternal state of the unbeliever. The passage, however, cannot be about final punishment. This is made clear for two reasons. The rich man is in Hades, not hell. That Hades is an intermediary place between death and judgement is made clear in Revelation 20:13, which describes how, "*death and Hades gave up the dead that were in them, and everyone was judged according to what they had done.*" Secondly, the rich man's brothers are still alive. This is another indication that the Final Judgement had not yet occurred. If the rich man was suffering eternally in hell, then he somehow got there long before he was supposed to.

So if Scripture doesn't teach it, logic doesn't necessitate it, God's character contradicts it, and skeptics are turned off by it, why does the evangelical Church still preach an errant view of hell? It is time to reconsider doctrines once they become destructive. For the sake of reaching the world with the love of God, this one should receive priority.

CHAPTER 5

Incorporating Modern Science into Theology

> Science without religion is lame. Religion without science is blind.
>
> —Albert Einstein

In the previous chapter, we spent some time opining on the final destiny of man. In this section, I would like to discuss his origin. There is perhaps no greater intellectual barrier to non-believers coming to a saving faith in our Lord than the perceived one between science and religion. Although not a taboo topic in Christian circles, a true and objective analysis of how the Bible reconciles itself to modern archeologic and genetic discoveries seems to be. As a result, the myth that we have to approach science and religion as two opposing subjects perpetuates itself. With that perpetuation comes the parallel stagnation of intellectuals accepting the Christian faith.

This chapter serves as an attempt to challenge honest Christian thinkers to evaluate what extent we (as the Church) have sacrificed accepting the realities of modern scientific discovery for fear of finding them in contrast to our exposition of Scripture. Put simply: are we stubbornly grasping a position on a peripheral issue in the Bible that may be preventing us from forming a bridge for scientific secularists to open their minds to God's truth?

The Debate from Darwin to Date

No subject of science better exemplifies this tension than that of Darwinian evolution. Alistair Donald presents a great summation of how, since the publication of Darwin's *On the Origin of Species* in 1859, the Church has been resistant to accept his claims.[1]

Interestingly, however, one of the first reactions of the Church was that of acceptance. Rev. Charles Kingsley, a historian, University professor and priest in the Church of England, upon receiving an advanced copy of Darwin's work gave a hands-down endorsement of it:

> *Dear Sir, I have to thank you for the unexpected honour of your book. That the Naturalist whom, of all naturalists living, I most wish to know and learn from, should have sent a scientist like me his book, encourages me at least to observe more carefully, and think more slowly.*

> *I am so poorly (in brain), that I fear I cannot read your book just now as I ought. All I have seen of it awes me; both with the heap of facts and the prestige of your name, and also with the clear intuition, that if you be right, I must give up much that I have believed and written.*
>
> *In that I care little. Let God be true, and every man a liar!*[2]

Further, recognizing the Church's overall historic rejection of Darwinian evolution, in 2008, Rev. Dr. Malcolm Brown, Director of Mission and Public Affairs for the Church of England, issued a letter of apology to the late author:

> *Charles Darwin: 200 years from your birth, the Church of England owes you an apology for misunderstanding you and, by getting our first reaction wrong, encouraging others to misunderstand you still. We try to practise the old virtues of 'faith seeking understanding' and hope that makes some amends.*[3]

Sandwiched in between these two men of God, however, the Church appears less than enthusiastic. Six years after the publication of Darwin's theory, the Victoria Institute was created to help reconcile Science with scripture. Many of the Institute's members challenged Darwin's theory.[4] In 1874, Charles Hodge, Principal of Princeton Seminary branded Darwinism "atheism."[5] (B. B. Warfield, his successor, however, endorsed a theistic version of Darwin's treatise.[6])

In 1887 Charles Spurgeon, the "Prince of Preachers," took an anti-Darwinian stance and subsequently received the support of hundreds of Baptist ministers.[7] Further, the ninety essays known as *The Fundamentals*, written in the early 1900s, that would be believed by many to have given rise to the Christian Fundamentalist movement, contained writings opposed to the theories found within the "Origins of Species."[8] Since then, many authors, thousands of preachers, and millions of believers have followed suit. Some responses to evolution, in fact, seem quite visceral:

> *"I believe that one day the Darwinian myth will be ranked the greatest deceit in the history of science."*
> —Søren Løvtrup[9]

> *"Scientists that go about teaching evolution as fact are great con-men, and the story they are telling may be the greatest hoax ever."* —N. J. Mitchell[10]

> *"Evolutionism is a fairy tale for grown-ups. This theory has helped nothing in the progress of science."*
> —Louis Bounoure[11]

What is the hang up for Christians? For those believers who honestly and intellectually believe the teachings of the Bible are not compatible with those of Darwinian evolution, on what do they base these opinions? The remainder of this chapter will examine three of the most common reasons why Christians find the teachings of evolution to be implausible. I will then attempt to provide a brief but adequate response to each reason.

Adam: The man, the myth...

Squaring the existence of a literal and specific "first man" (Adam) with Darwin's theory of evolution has always been a nonstarter for most Christians. If God created Adam "from the dust of the ground"[12] and Eve from "one of [his] ribs"[13] then what room could there possibly have been for the evolutionary process? Indeed, many authors have gone to great lengths defending either side of the issue, but for the purpose of keeping our discussion to a "survey of ideas," I will simply propose two responses to the traditional evangelical stance.

First, every sentence of the creation texts found in Genesis 1 and 2 can be true and reconciled with a slow development of the *homo sapiens* species over time. Denis Alexander, in his book "Creation or Evolution: Do we have to Choose," proposes that anatomically modern humans have been in existence for ~200,000 years and were the result of over 3.6 billion years of evolutionary process.[14] The mention of Adam and Eve in first two chapters of the Bible simply represents the time of God's choosing when He selected two of them to whom to reveal Himself and make them spiritually distinct. Alexander calls this event the advent of *homo divinus*... and the remainder of Genesis plays out: Sin infects the human race after the "law of the tree" is given and Christ is sent to deliver God's chosen creation from their iniquities.

One common objection to Alexander's proposal may be that, "if Adam co-existed with millions of other *homo sapiens*, then how can we all be direct descendants of his line (as Scripture clearly states is the case)?" This can be easily answered through God's limitation of allowing only eight on the ark.

This interpretation of the creation text *does* in fact prevent us from taking all its prose literally (since Adam was actually a decedent of another *homo sapiens* and not "the dust of the ground"). However, I would submit, no biblical scholar can honestly approach Genesis from a purely literal perspective. Who amongst us believes God literally walked in the Garden with Adam and Eve? Or who would argue God did not really know where Adam was when He asked?[15] Further, many widely respected Christian authors readily concede (based on fossil records, earth layers, etc.) creation could not have taken place in a literal seven-day period. Why then does drawing the next logical conclusion appear as such an anathema?

Second, accepting evolution as a plausible theory does not preclude the involvement of God's creative hand over the past 3.6 billion years. Doesn't it do quite the opposite? A theistic evolutionary approach allows us to view God as less of a "magician" and more of a master creator, who weaves his creative influence throughout the development of millions of species over billions of years. What a mind blowing and theologically freeing thought!

The Eye of the Storm

I do not want my passion on this issue to be mistaken for certainty. I do not for a moment assume that either the science is closed or that the Bible is clearly in favor of the argument of the validity of Darwin's theory of evolution. My desire here is simply to prompt thinking where minds might be closed. In researching this chapter, I read some key, current books on this issue, but I also went back to my personal library to a shelf of dusty, less modern books. On this shelf, I found a title written by the great "Bible Answer Man" of the 1990s, Hank Hanegraaff, ambitiously named "The Face that Demonstrates the Farce of Evolution." As I picked it up and thumbed through it, memories started to return of my many well-intentioned debates with high school peers and teachers regarding just how ridiculous I thought it was for an intellectual to believe in the unproven theory of evolution. My lynch-pin argument was found within the illustration of the complexity of the human eye. I would proudly point out to surrounding skeptics, "the human eye attaches to the brain through tens of thousands of neuronal connections. If any one of these connections was missing, we would be blinded. So you see, the eye could not have slowly developed over time. We either see or we do not see. God either created it, or it happened by improbable chance."

Across from his explanation of the unlikelihood of the chance development of the human eye, Hanegraaf placed a picture of the *Last Supper* by Leonardo da Vinci. "Imagine the assertion that [this picture] painted itself,"[16] he suggests. Again, implying that you either have a *Last Supper* painting or have no painting at all. There can be no in-betweens.

The problem is that modern science can now trace back over millions of years of fossils and genetic records the detailed development of the human eye. Alexander points out that many single-cell organisms have light-detecting areas known as "eyespots". These spots can detect luminescence but fail to be able to detect the direction from where the light comes. So, next in evolutionary history were organisms that contained the same light-sensitive eyespots, but they were indented into the surface of the subject. This indentation allowed for the direction of light to be ascertained. These "pit eyes," as Alexander explains, exist in some flatworms and are thought to have developed in the Cambrian era some 540 million years ago. "Pinhole-lens eyes" developed thereafter, which allowed for imaging but since they lacked a cornea or lens, allowed only for poor resolution. The eye continued to develop over ~400,000 generations, increasing in complexity over time into the remarkable specimen we have today.[17]

Reading Alexander's book gave me good reason to question some of the arguments made by traditional creationists. What's more is that the assertion that either evolution is true or the Bible is true, again, is a false dichotomy. Why can't there be both? Why not let God be the God of the Evolutionary Process?

A Truly Dynamic Argument

The last objection to Darwin's theory I will mention in this chapter involves the second Law of Thermodynamics. Simply put, this law states that entropy will always increase. In other words, a system will always go from less chaos to more chaos, from more order to less order, or from more energy to less energy. The creationist's argument goes something like, "If order is lost over time, how can anything evolve or improve? How can a more complex and sophisticated being develop from one less endowed? If thermodynamics is a 'law,' certainly that has to trump unproven science that is stuck in theory."

The implication here is that the tenants found within the theory of evolution stand contradictory to those found within the law of thermodynamics, but this simply is not the case. *The key to understanding thermodynamics is the consideration that the law only applies to a closed system.* There are plenty of examples in which order can be increased within one part of a system but decreased overall. I attend a church where one of our lead pastors constantly brags about his amazing wood pile. He loves to chop wood and add to its beauty, all the while knowing he will eventually enjoy the warmth his wood will provide during the cold winter months. Herein, we have two examples of *increased* order:

#1 Pastor Ryan is able to take an unorganized pile of wood and make it look organized and attractive.

#2 The ambient temperature is going from hot to cold (a decrease in molecular movement, that would by definition imply a decrease in entropy).

Nonetheless, the second law of thermodynamics is not broken. This is because both are examples of activities within a greater system. In example #1, Pastor Ryan expended energy in creating his woodpile. The logs were moved from one place to another, but his sweat energy was lost to his environment. Overall, entropy increased. In example #2, the weather got colder in his neighborhood, but since Ryan's neck of the woods is part of a greater global system, fear not. The sun beats heavily on the Earth somewhere else, and the law of thermodynamics remains in place.

It is easy to see how these examples might translate to a better understanding of evolution. At times, events might occur that increase order. An "eye spot" may develop into a human eye over time. A heart may develop that more efficiently pumps blood throughout a body. A marine-based life form may develop the capability of surviving on land. These happenings are permissible as long as the overall entropy of the total system is maintained or increased, and this is the case since energy is expended in each step of the evolutionary process.

What Difference Does It Make?

While I have come to lean towards supporting a theistic evolutionary process, I am far from certain I am correct. What I am certain of is that many who do not follow Christ are turned off by an approach to science that ignores facts already in evidence. They are unwilling to forsake what they regard as truth for what they view as an ancient book, the teachings of which (so they are told) contradict the laws of nature the book's Protagonist is said to have created!

Why should we force anyone to choose between science and faith, especially when no one can make the argument that any major tenants of Christianity hang in the balance! The flip-side also true. Why tie the hands of the evangelist when he is reaching out to a non-Christian who happens to be an ardent opponent of creationism?

Would we not much rather gladly proclaim to said opponent that his objections are no barrier to a saving faith in our Lord? Indeed, the Christian faith could stand to choose one less hill to die on.

CHAPTER 6

The Importance of Avoiding Bibliolatry

"Contradiction is not a sign of falsity nor lack of contradiction a sign of truth."

—Blaise Pascal

Despite countless areas of disagreement among evangelicals, there are three major tenants considered fundamental to our beliefs: the Trinity, salvation by grace through faith, and the inspiration of Scripture. Throughout history, all three have been the focus of attack. Nonetheless, Christians have made no compromise in their steadfast defenses. As I enter into the next chapter of a book that has questioned many historically upheld theological norms, the reader might be concerned I am going to aim fire at one of the above doctrines as an attempted "grand finale". The reader may be assured that this is the opposite of my intentions.

However, the lattermost tenant (the inspiration of Scripture) *is* under cultural attack and the most common evangelical arguments in rebuttal are serving to further the perceived divide between faith and logic. The contents of this chapter serve as a brief summary of the substance of that attack and (it is my hope) will provide a challenge to how the issue is frequently addressed.

The Nature of the Battle

Let's begin by stating the obvious: non-believers do not hold the Bible in the same esteem as we do. They have not been indoctrinated with the concept that "God wrote the Bible" and that to criticize its contents is beyond the boundaries of mere mortals. They apply the same tests of trustworthiness and validity to the Bible as they might to any historical writing, and no bias created by reverence influences their conclusions.

What's more, they observe the evangelical's steadfast adoration of the Ancient Text with curiosity. "It's a good book… a great book, even," they might opine, "but who can believe that God wrote a book that is imperfect?" They may even be able to cite some historic contradictions. Those found within the various accounts of the crucifixion in the four Gospels will serve as an illustration here:

1. **What color robe Jesus was given?**

    Matthew 27:28: They stripped off his clothes and put a **scarlet robe** on him.

John 19:2: The soldiers made a crown out of thorny branches and put it on his head; then they put a **purple robe** on him.

2. Who was it that carried Jesus' cross?

Mark 15:20b-22: ... Then they led him out to crucify him. On the way they met a man named **Simon**, who was coming into the city from the country, and the soldiers forced him to carry Jesus' cross... They took Jesus to a place called Golgotha, which means "The Place of the Skull".

John 19:16-17: Then Pilate handed Jesus over to them to be crucified. So they took charge of **Jesus**. He went out, carrying his cross, and came to "The Place of the Skull", as it is called.

3. When was Jesus crucified?

Mark 15:25: It was **9 o'clock** in the morning when they crucified him.

John 19:14-16: It was then almost **noon** of the day before the Passover. Pilate said to the people, "Here is your king!". They shouted back, "Kill him! Kill him! Crucify him!"... then Pilate handed Jesus over to them to be crucified.

4. **What were the Centurion's words at the cross?**

   Matthew 27:54: When the army officer and the soldiers with him who were watching Jesus saw the earthquake and everything else that happened, they were terrified and said, **"He really was the Son of God!"**

   Luke 23:47: The army officer saw what had happened, and he praised God, saying, **"Certainly he was a good man!"**

5. **What were Jesus' last words on the cross?**

   Matthew 27:46b: Eli, Eli, lama sabachtani? That is to say, **My God, My God, why did you abandon me?**

   Luke 23:46: Father, in your hand I place my spirit.

   John 19:30: It is finished.

The best response for the believer to confrontation on these issues is not to try to reconcile the irreconcilable. Indeed, asking the non-believer to check his brain at the door on this issue is what has, for centuries, been an unnecessary stumbling block to faith for many intellectuals. It is my firm belief that the most persuasive response is to instead educate the non-believer on the mode which God used to allow His word to be written.

Is the Bible God-Inspired?

Absolutely. 2 Tim 3:16 clearly and succinctly states that "All Scripture is God-breathed and is useful for teaching, rebuking, correcting, and training in righteousness." So at least Paul the Apostle believed it was. Jesus also shared this viewpoint. He is often seen quoting passages of the Old Testament and holding them in supreme authority (Math 19:7, Math 22:29, Mark 7:6, etc.). But does *inspiration* have to equal *inerrancy?*

Failing to delineate a clear distinction between these two concepts is what has resulted in great confusion during centuries of battle for wide adoption of the Bible as intellectually and existentially relevant to a modern culture. On one extreme, we have believers arguing "*God wrote the Bible. Therefore, it's perfect. And if it's perfect, there can be no mistakes.*" It is this group of people who feel the need to "justify" any discrepancy found. Let's briefly look at the translational sleight of hand found in the NIV that was performed in order to reconcile Acts 9:7 with Acts 22:9.

Both passages describe Paul's vision of Christ while on the road to Damascus. In 9:7, Paul's companions heard Jesus' voice but saw no one. "The men traveling with Saul stood there speechless. They heard the sound but did not see anyone." In 22:9, as Paul recounts his conversion experience, his group saw the light, but did not hear "the voice speaking to [Paul]." Now what was or wasn't seen presents no problem for defenders of inerrancy. Perhaps Paul's companions saw a light (22:9) but failed to see anyone specifically (9:7). There is no need for both passages to include all the details. What is more problematic is that one verse (9:7) has Paul's fellow travelers hearing Jesus and one has them hearing nothing. Clearly, both cannot be true. As Peter Enns states in his contribution to the book "Five Views on Biblical Inerrancy":

> *Unlike the synoptic problem in the Gospels and the historical books of the Old Testament (Kings and Chronicles), which is explained on the basis of the different historical settings, audiences, and perspectives of the authors, this discrepancy in Acts is within the same book and by the same author, and so poses a different sort of challenge to inerrancy.*[1]

In order to reconcile these differing accounts, the NIV translates 22:9 to say that Paul's companions "did not *understand* (emphasis mine) the voice". Obviously there is no contradiction if the group "heard the voice" in one passage yet "did not understand" it in the next. But there is no precedent in the Greek to translate "akouo" (to hear/listen) followed by "phone" (sound/voice) as anything other than "to hear [or listen to] the sound [or voice]". Look to John 10:3,

16, 27 and John 18:37 as examples in which this translational liberty isn't taken. It is apparent that the translators felt the need to make these two conflicting passages mesh.

On the other extreme, opposite from the inerrancy defenders, are those who claim the Bible could not possibly have been inspired by God in light of its handful of contradictions. It is this group of skeptics that Christians unnecessarily isolate by their refusal to find common ground.

Mode of Inspiration

If the Bible is inspired, even God-breathed, how can we reconcile the fact that it is not without error? The answer is easy when you consider the vessel God chose to use in order to communicate His word: mankind.

Just like, as Christians, we are called to share God's truth with those who have yet to accept the graces of God, so were the writers called to deliver the truth of God in written form. It is very hard to make the argument that the validity of the message is compromised simply because the messenger is imperfect. One can witness the transformative work God does through imperfect people on a daily, even moment-by-moment basis. Why would we think His choice to work the same way in written form at all strange, let alone unacceptable?

Why even make a big deal out of defending inerrancy in the first place? No one would argue that any significant teaching of the Bible is affected by the presence of its few inconsistencies. Take, for example, the above discrepancies presented regarding the crucifixion story of Jesus. If Matthew remembers Jesus' robe as being scarlet and John said it was purple, who cares? The greater story that Christ was crucified and eventually raised from the dead remains unaffected.

Besides, what if by referencing Christ's scarlet robe, Matthew wanted to emphasize that Jesus was a sacrificial lamb to his predominantly Jewish audience? John could have very well desired to bring to light Jesus the dying King, when speaking of his purple attire. This brief survey of topics bears no opportunity to dive deeper into the nuances of first century story-telling, but suffice it to say the cultural differences also need to be taken into account when analyzing the truths of Scripture.

What is bibliolatry?

Simply defined, bibliolatry is the worship of the Bible. The root of the fervency most Christians have in defending the Bible as inerrant is the tendency to believe the Bible is itself divine. Many Christians, though they would never say it, hold the Bible at such a high elevation, it succeeds to the position of almost being a fourth Person of the Trinity; it is as if poking holes in the Bible was equivalent to tearing down the Godhead itself.

We need to realize that God chose the texts found in the Bible to be the written vessels He would use to communicate timeless truths to the world, and that, while He could have sent down golden tablets to be found in a forest, He decided to use fallible man as scribes for His Word.

Evangelism aside, it can be quite dangerous for the believer to hold the Bible in higher regard than it was intended. We do not worship a text. We worship the great God and Creator of heaven and earth!

So what should our response be?

In a world that is now more than ever in need of the love of our Lord and Savior, creating yet another intellectual barrier for those that need Him to come to a salvific faith in Christ does our message a great disservice. Some, in light of the above examples of biblical inconsistencies, may choose not to reject the word "inerrancy". Instead, they may desire to redefine it in a way that accommodates the facts at hand. Clark Pinnock does this in his book "The Scripture Principle." This may make some more comfortable, but it isn't helpful and confuses the issue. (Dare I say I am to the left of Pinnock on this.) The Bible is the most powerful tool believers have to share God's love and introduce His truth to the world. Let us be careful to use it… and represent it, as intended.

CHAPTER 7

Escaping Evangelical Elitism

"In your relationships with one another, have the same attitude of mind that Christ had: Who, being in very nature God, did not consider equality with God something to be used to his own advantage; rather he made himself nothing by taking on the very nature of a servant..."

—Philippians 2: 5-7

Jesus, the Way the Truth

Making the decision to live a life committed to God, one that recognizes Jesus as both Lord and Savior, is both humbling and invigorating at the same time. For someone who believes that Jesus provides the only pathway to eternal life, it is easy to understand why she would desire to see others join in entering that blessed hope. Certainly it is the Holy Spirit that has instilled in her a heart for the world and desire to see "not one man perish but come to repentance".[1]

It is this same zeal, however, that can lead many well-intentioned faithful to an "us vs. them" mentality that does not at all reflect the heart of God. To be sure, we are no longer in the days of the Crusades, and the outpouring of this attitude is a bit more insidious than it used to be. But it is just as prevalent. The turn or burn street or tele-evangelist, the one who dons the religious gotcha-trope bumper sticker, and the social media debate enthusiast provide a mere a sampling of more contemporary self-aggrandizing proselytization techniques. These methods serve little to convey God's love and mostly to widen the separation between what inevitably comes to be seen as two classes of people, the "chosen" and the "sinner".

"Black or white", "in or out", "lost or found". Classification begets judgement and judgement begets elitism, whether explicit or hidden. As followers of Christ, we are not called to partake in such categorization. Sharing the heart of God with a world in need of His love is a noble task indeed. (In fact, as Christ followers, it is our calling.) But we should never err to assume that the Church of God has exclusive access to the truths of God. In fact, it is when this attitude takes root that we are most likely to witness ripe fields turn into barren wastelands.

Seekers not Targets

I fully confess my own proclivity towards this way of thinking. As a young evangelical, I was brought up in an environment in which "winning souls" was paramount and equated to how effectively one was being used by God to achieve His ends. I call this the "dotted line" mentality, since the salvific box was checked if you could get the vagabond sinner to sign off on praying *the prayer* of salvation. Whether it was in the Sunday church pew or the weekly meeting of Campus Crusade for Christ, watching the tally grow often seemed prioritized over the actual goal, which is the cultivation of a changed life.

Not that any mode of evangelism I participated in was inherently bad. (Indeed, Paul states "whether from false motives or true, the gospel is preached. And because of this I rejoice."[2]) But my heart was not always aligned true to God's. Non-Christians were often targets, not co-equal creations on their own pathway towards truth. And I honestly believe I inhibited as many journeys as I aided at times by my approach to evangelism. Knocking on dorm room doors, I had just as many shut in my face then productive conversations as I interrupted Mario Kart races armed with my Four Spiritual Laws book and Kennedy questions.[3] Walking up and down Panama City Beach on Spring Break, I'm sure I made more eyes roll than hearts dance as I tried to stir God-time into mixed drinks. It is regretfully only in retrospect that I can see why little fruit was bared during these times.

I can honestly say that my most impactful moments as an evangelist have come when an actual relationship preceded a conversation and true concern replaced any attempts to contrive. More than ever before, my mentality in speaking with and relating to a non-Christian is identical to my approach to relating to a fellow believer. Very few people wake up in the morning plotting the evil they wish to propagate upon the world, delighting in damnation as they embrace the wrong-headedness of their belief system. Most, religious or not, try to live their best lives, love people and do good. This is the prevenient grace of God at work. It is the common ground we all share as seekers of truth, and we should be just as mindful of what God wants to teach us through them as we are of wanting to convince anyone to believe what we do.

A Wideness of Grace

I believe the Christian, fearing the ultimate demise of the lost, can take some comfort in knowing that God is already at work far before any explicit gospel message is preached. In fact, I would argue that the contrasting concept of soteriological particularism (the idea that man cannot be saved outside of the explicit hearing and accepting of the gospel message) is a primary culprit in propagating evangelical elitism.

No Other Name

Though not a dominant view outside of their circles, many evangelicals believe that it is impossible to receive God's offering of eternal life outside of the above parenthetic scenario. Indeed, evangelicals are right in claiming that "there is no other name under heaven given to mankind by which we must be saved."[4] But does that mean the salvation cannot be found where the name of Jesus is not known or understood? Traditionally, evangelicalism has answered in the affirmative.

But particularism seems to be more of an inference than an explicit teaching from the Bible. Proof texts can be cited:

Acts 4:12- quoted above

Romans 10:9- *If you declare with your mouth, "Jesus is Lord," and believe in your heart that God raised him from the dead, you will be saved.*

John 3:16- *For God so loved the world that he gave his one and only Son, that whoever believes in him shall not perish but him eternal life.*

But is salvation offered to all yet existentially limited to a select few throughout history? And if so, how can this outcome reflect the heart of God? A deeper dive into the subject gives plenty of evidence that righteousness with God is more widely available.

Evangelical Inclusivism

Evangelical inclusivism is the concept that, while Jesus Christ is the One who provides the means of salvation, it is possible for eternal life to be granted to one who does not receive Jesus by name. Paul seems to be speaking to this scenario specifically when in Romans 1 he states:

"The wrath of God is being revealed from heaven against all the godlessness and wickedness of human beings who suppress the truth by their wickedness, since what may be known about God is plain to them, because God has made it plain to them. For since the creation of the world God's invisible qualities-his eternal power and divine nature- have been clearly seen, being understood from what has been made, so that people are without excuse.[5]*"*

If man can be held accountable for disobedience by the evidence within nature provided to them, surely they can be justified through the same revelation.

Further, we can see examples within Scripture of men considered righteous who were not follows of Jesus. Acts 10 speaks of the centurion, Cornelius:

"He and all his family were devout and God-fearing; he gave generously to those in need and prayed to God regularly."[6] Further, his *"prayers and gifts to the poor* [had] *come up as a memorial offering before God."*[7]

That Cornelius had no explicit revelation of Jesus is made clear by the call Peter was given to go preach at his house. And the lesson Peter was consequentially taught after initially resisting communion with the gentile illustrates that, "*God does not show favoritism but accepts those from every nation who fear him and do what is right.*"[8]

Another example is found in Genesis with the pagan priest Melchizedek. His cameo is quite brief, but the lesson taught nonetheless impactful:

> *After Abram returned from defeating Kedorlaomer and the kings allied with him, the king of Sodom came out to meet him in the Valley of Shaveh (that is, the King's Valley). Then Melchizedek king of Salem brought out bread and wine. He was priest of God Most High, and he blessed Abram, saying, "Blessed be Abram by God Most High, Creator of heaven and earth. And praise be to God Most High, who delivered your enemies into your hand." Then Abram gave him a tenth of everything.*[9]

Melchizedek blesses Abraham in the name of his God, *El Elyon*. In return, Abraham accepts the blessing and tithes to Melchizedek in the name of *Yahweh*. The exchange seems to draw an equivalence between the two divinities. Abraham does not seek to evangelize Melchizedek; rather, he accepts the blessing as from his own God. What an example of mutual respect and fellowship that is rarely seen between the evangelical and his "gospel-deprived" prey!

The most conclusive evidence of evangelical inclusivism can simply be found within the Old Testament as a body of work. It cannot be logically argued that all the saints of old knew the name of Jesus, let alone His future work on the cross. Nor can it be acceptably concluded that salvation was only allotted post 32 AD.

I do not want the reader to understand the above as an argument for religious pluralism. The evangelical inclusivist affirms that it is only by the work of Christ that the escape from judgement is possible. Nor am I trying to say all religious groups simply worship the God of the Bible by another name. Clearly, there are many destructive and cultish sects in the world that have no right to be positioned alongside the hearts of the well-intended. It is simply my aim for the reader to leave open the possibility, even likelihood, that there are those seekers who are not Christian in name but who worship God, and whose worship is accepted by Him. Indeed, evangelism would take on a whole new and fruitful light if approached with this in mind.

A Relational Approach

Widely respected within the Open community, Dr. Thomas Oord has done a lot of work to foster productive dialogue among members of diverse faith traditions. His Center for Open and Relational Theology (c4ort.com) serves as a resource center and virtual networking launch pad for any who would affirm two basic principles: that "God experiences time moment by moment (is open)" and that "God, us and creation relate, so that everyone gives and receives (is relational)".[10] While theological differences matter, as Dr. Oord affirms, it is the call of the believer to partake in the heart and love of God. We are to commune, as Jesus did, not only with the like-minded, but with any who would seek truth. We are to give what God has made plain to us and to accept what God has illuminated for others. And we are to do so with discernment, against the revelation in Scripture already given, but mostly with a joyful love that allows the grace of God to flourish in a world too often characterized by its darkness.

CHAPTER 8

Conclusion - The Role of Theology in Modern Discourse

This brief survey of topics has served to draw attention to some key areas in which modern evangelicalism has held onto traditional views of God and the Bible to the detriment of achieving its ultimate purpose: propagating a faith that is real, affectual, and saving to a non-believing world. In the preceding chapters, vast ground was covered in a condensed fashion. In an age in which emphasis on emotion often overrules the legitimacy of logical discussion, we are left with one final question: "Why does any of this matter?"

One might be tempted to opine, "I leave theology up to the theologians. What matters to me is my relationship with God and I care much less about how it all works."

These statements represent the unfortunate mindset for the majority of the Church. For those of us who are theologically inclined (a safe assumption on my part, you would not have made it this far into my book if you were not), it is our responsibility to set the tone for the importance of studying the character and governance of God. This is the case for several reasons.

#1 Your beliefs about God come from somewhere, often not the Bible

One who chooses not to study theology at least on some level makes a real decision (consciously or not) to surrender their access to knowledge of the divine to those who are willing to study for them. Put more simply, if you choose not to study God, someone will study Him for you… and tell you what to believe.

Nearly every believer has an opinion of how God "works" and of who God is, but very few can explain why they believe what they do. They are not able to separate out what they have been taught during Sunday school from what the Bible actually says. And this is exactly how misinformation becomes generational. It is precisely how a believer who knows for a fact that the God of the Bible is loving and good may at the same time be convinced that He would allow someone to be tormented for eternity for refusing to also believe. It's the same reason why a believer may mourn the pain and suffering of a close relative while at the same time having faith that God really wants the suffering to take place, if only for a "greater good".

Those who choose not to constructively analyze their belief systems for the sake of soundness of doctrine do themselves a disservice and, more detrimentally, fail to accurately portray a God of love to a world in need.

#2 Theology allows us to reconcile belief and action

Failing to construct a proper theological model does not just lead to intellectual inconsistencies, it often results in a clear dichotomy between the intellectual and the existential. In other words, the Christ follower's beliefs may not be in line with her actions. For example, most believers would say that nothing happens outside the will of God. However, the same people ardently pray like their intercession makes a difference. Most believers would say that God already knows who among His creation will ultimately be saved in the end. Yet the aim of the same evangelical is to share Christ at every opportunity lest he miss the chance to bring someone closer to God. Proper theology **must** reconcile these inconsistencies.

#3 We become more adept at sharing our faith

1 Peter 3:15 says to, "Always be prepared to give an answer to everyone who asks you to give the reason for the hope

that you have." A mind in tune to and knowledgeable about God will be able to convey God's love to those in need of it in a much more intelligible way. We have all met skeptics who say they cannot believe in God because He does not make sense to them. Most of those opposed to or agnostic towards faith are unwilling to simply accept the claims of Christianity at face value. It is not the "what" they are ignorant of; they need a clear presentation of the "why". A student of the faith will be able to meet that sacred call.

And not only will she be able to respond to an opportunity presented, but she will be able to do so in a way that reflects the heart of the God she pursues. As detailed in the previous chapter, right words can be presented in destructive ways. May we be those who rightly handle the word of truth.

#4 God finds joy in those who seek after Him

Further, the study of God is important because God says it is.

And He finds great satisfaction when His children yearn to know Him.

> **Proverbs 8:17**- *I love those who love me and those who seek me find me.*
>
> **Hebrews 11:6**-*And without faith it is impossible to please God, because anyone who comes to him must*

believe that he exists and that he rewards those who earnestly seek him.

Psalms 14:2-*The LORD looks down from heaven on all mankind to see if there are any who understand, any who seek God.*

Just as it is the honor of the groom to spend a lifetime seeking to know and understand the bride, and just as that pursuit draws the two ever closer, so it is with our relationship with God. I am convinced there are many truths about God that He leaves purposefully unclear so we will find greater contentment in the journey towards the answer. This is theology.

#5 Our own wonderment is deepened

This is even true if we cannot walk away in full agreement with the mode of theology being studied. Recently, I have endeavored to learn more about Process Theology, reading Whitehead, Cobb, Measle and more. As an open theist, I find a lot in common, in fact inspiring, about the relational God they present. To the process theist, God is immanent, experiential and the ultimate partner with mankind in bringing about the best possible future.

The process God is not independent of but interdependent with creation, as impacted by it as He is able to effect it. Creation was not *ex nihilo,* and no coercion is able to be propagated upon it. Instead, the universe is simply the canvas upon which God has been painting since time eternal and it is his ultimate desire for beauty to be brought about and not destroyed by evil. To that end, he works day and night.

While I cannot ultimately agree with the involuntary interdependence presented within process thought and the emphasis placed on Whiteheadian philosophy over sound scriptural exegesis, I have taken away a much deeper appreciation of creation than I have had previously. If the earth is all we have (eschatology has next to no place in process theism) then our purpose is to preserve and prepare it for future generations. Indeed, sound ecology being paramount is a far cry from the "it's all going to burn anyway" thinking of many traditional evangelicals. What a breath of fresh air!

In the end...

In the end, my challenge to the reader is this: Pursue the knowledge of who God is because it is our duty and our privilege. Challenge yourself to consider what has been presented in the preceding chapters and consider the importance of accurately portraying God to the world. And be willing to be the shipmate who works to correct the direction of a craft that has strayed off course. God has entrusted the vessel of His Church with the great responsibility of bringing His children home. We should seek to be found worthy of this great call.

REFERENCES

Acknowledgements
1. Arminian compatibilists hold to the philosophy the free will and divine foreknowledge can coexist.

Preface
1. Bible. New International Version.1 Tim 1:16
2. Bible. New International Version. 1 Peter 5:13
3. Bible. New International Version. James 1:6
4. Bible. New International Version. 2 Corinthians 5:20
5. I refer here to the writing of *The Openness of God* by Pinnock, et al. which was the first major work to introduce the theology of open theism.
6. Reformed theology has for decades been considered the dominant view of Christian scholarship
7. David Bassinger. The Case for Free Will Theism.
8. Clark Pinnock. The Openness of God. Systematic Theology. 104

Chapter 1: How Hellenism Poisoned the Well
1. Gerald Friedlander. Hellenism and Christianity. 26-27.
2. Everett Ferguson. Backgrounds of Early Christianity. 327-330.
3. Ibid 333.

4. Ibid 330-333.
5. John Sanders. The Openness of God. Historical Considerations. 62-63
6. Everett Ferguson. Backgrounds of Early Christianity. 334.
7. Ibid 354.
8. Ibid 359.
9. John Sanders. The Openness of God. Historical Considerations. 67
10. Everett Ferguson. Backgrounds of Early Christianity. 360; Ibid 67
11. Everett Ferguson. Backgrounds of Early Christianity. 358
12. Ibid 370-378.
13. John Sanders. The Openness of God. Historical Considerations. 69
14. http://www.britannica.com/EBchecked/topic/456612/PhiloJudaeus accessed 6/1/15
15. Everett Ferguson. Backgrounds of Early Christianity. 479
16. John Sanders. The Openness of God. Historical Considerations. 70-71
17. Everett Ferguson. Backgrounds of Early Christianity. 483
18. http://plato.stanford.edu/entries/augustine/accessed 6/1/15.
19. John Sanders. The Openness of God. Historical Considerations. 80
20. The Confessions of Saint Augustine. Augustine. Book 7. Chapter 11.
21. Ibid. Book 13. Chapter 16.
22. http://calvinistinternational.com/2014/01/30/augustinecompassion- impassibility/accessed 6/1/15.
23. The Confessions of Saint Augustine. Augustine. Book 11. Chapter 18.
24. On Faith, Hope and Love. Augustine. Chapter 102.

Chapter 2: How God Ordained Free Choice

1. Bible. New International Version. Galations 2:11-21
2. Mildred Bangs Wynkoop. Foundations of Wesleyan-Arminian Theology. 18
3. Ibid. 24-34
4. Ibid. 35
5. Ibid. 36
6. Ibid. 42
7. Ibid 59
8. Ibid 39
9. R. C. Sproul. What is Reformed Theology. 175
10. Bible. New International Version. Genesis 25:29-34, Genesis 36, 2 Chronicles 21:10
11. Ibid. 1 Timothy 2:4
12. William Hasker. God, Time and Knowledge. 69.
13. Jon Tal Murphree. Divine Paradoxes. 49-56.

Chapter 3: The Problem of the Problem of Pain

1. C. S. Lewis. The Problem of Pain. 14
2. John Sanders. Openness of God. Historical Considerations. 67
3. Augustine. On Free Will. 3.68
4. Gregory Boyd. Is God to Blame. 41-60
5. Bible. New International Version. Matthew 21:12
6. Ibid. John 11:1-44
7. Ibid. Matthew 27:32-56
8. Ibid. Matthew 20:28
9. Ibid. Luke 4:18
10. Ibid. John 12:32

Chapter 4: Is Eternal Suffering for the Masses?

1. Bible. New International Version. 1 John 4:8
2. Ibid. Romans 6:23
3. Plato. Phaedo. 69e-84b
4. Augustine. City of God. Chapter 23
5. John Calvin. Psychopannychia
6. Bible. New International Version. Genesis 3:22

Chapter 5: Incorporating Modern Science into Theology

1. Alistair Donald. Should Christians Embrace Evolution. Evolution and the Church. 15-19
2. http://www.evolutionnews.org/2011/darwins_first_theist_charles_k o 49831.html. Accessed 6.26.16
3. http://www.telegraph.co.uk/news/religion/2910447/CharlesDarwin-to-receive-apology-from-the-Church-of-England-forrejecting-evolution.html. Accessed 6.26.16
4. Alistair Donald. Should Christians Embrace Evolution. Evolution and the Church. 16-17
5. Charles Hodge. What is Darwinism? And Other Writing on Science and Religion. 177
6. David Livingstone. B.B. Warfield: A Biblical Inerrantist as Evolutionist. 14
7. Alistair Donald. Should Christians Embrace Evolution. Evolution and the Church. 16-17
8. Ibid. 18
9. Soren Lovtrup. Darwinism: The Refutation of a Myth. 422
10. N. J. Mitchell. Dr. T. N. Tahmisian Evolution and the Emperor's New Clothes. Title page
11. Louis Bounoure. The Advocate. March-8-1984. 17
12. Bible. New International Version. Genesis 2:7

13. Ibid. Genesis 2:21
14. Denis Alexander: Creation or Evolution: Do We Have to Choose?. 107, 236
15. Bible. New International Version. Genesis 3:9
16. Hank Hanegraaf. The Face that Demonstrates the Farce of Evolution. 60
17. Denis Alexander: Creation or Evolution: Do We Have to Choose? 167-173

Chapter 6: The Importance of Avoiding Bibliolatry

1. Peter Enns. Five Views on Biblical Inerrancy. 99

Chapter 7: Escaping Evangelical Elitism

1. Bible. New International Version. 2 Peter 3:9
2. Ibid. Philippians 1:18
3. www.evangelismexplosion.org Accessed 10-26-21
4. Bible. New International Version. Acts 4:12
5. Ibid. Romans 1:18-20
6. Ibid. Acts 10:2
7. Ibid. Acts 10:5
8. Ibid. Acts 10:34
9. Ibid. Genesis 14: 17-20
10. www.c4ort.com Accessed 10-26-21

ALSO FROM
SacraSage Press...

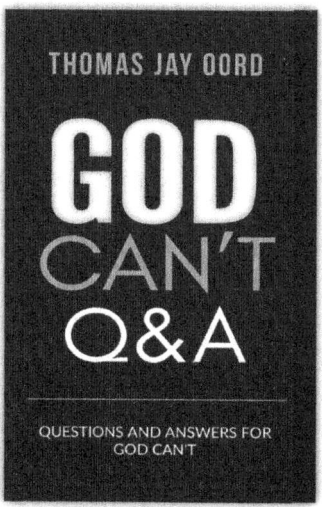

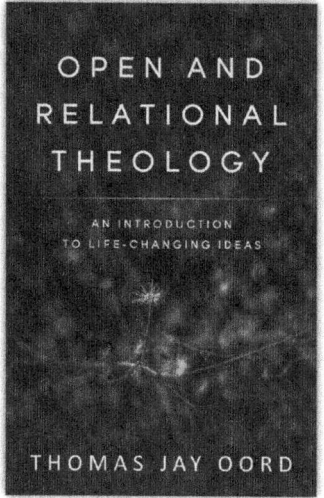

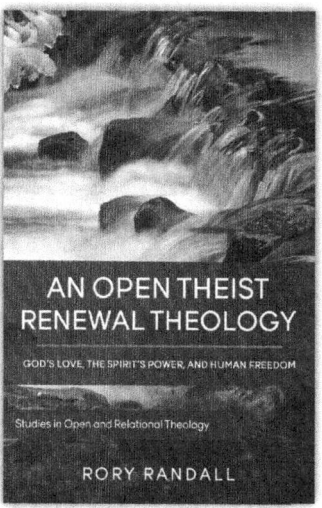

God Can't
THOMAS JAY OORD

God Can't Q&A
THOMAS JAY OORD
QUESTIONS AND ANSWERS FOR GOD CAN'T

Open and Relational Theology
AN INTRODUCTION TO LIFE-CHANGING IDEAS
THOMAS JAY OORD

An Open Theist Renewal Theology
GOD'S LOVE, THE SPIRIT'S POWER, AND HUMAN FREEDOM
Studies in Open and Relational Theology
RORY RANDALL

SACRASAGEPRESS.COM

ALSO FROM SacraSage Press...

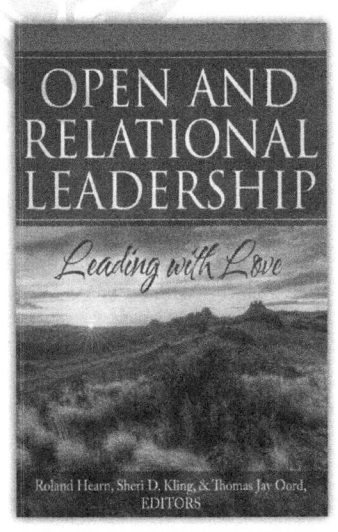

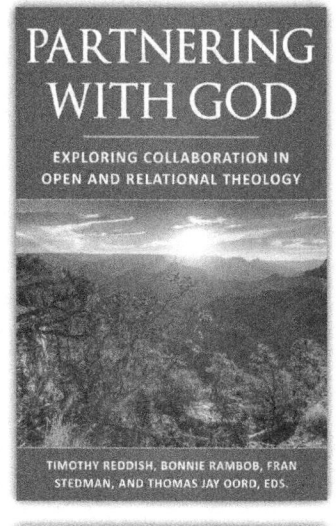

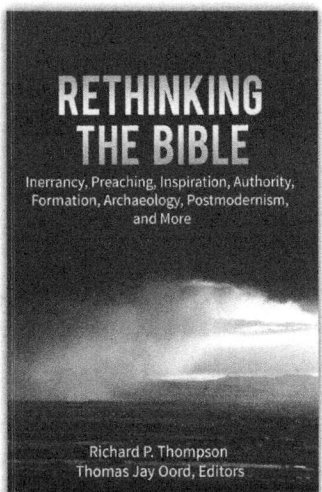

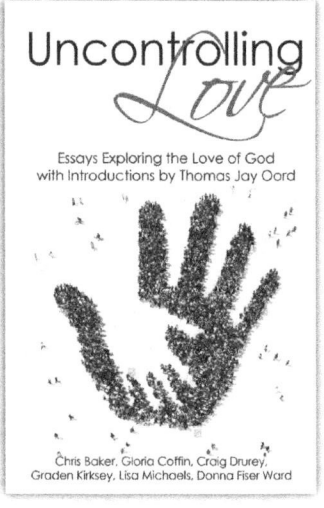

OPEN AND RELATIONAL LEADERSHIP: Leading with Love
Roland Hearn, Sheri D. Kling, & Thomas Jay Oord, EDITORS

PARTNERING WITH GOD: EXPLORING COLLABORATION IN OPEN AND RELATIONAL THEOLOGY
TIMOTHY REDDISH, BONNIE RAMBOB, FRAN STEDMAN, AND THOMAS JAY OORD, EDS.

RETHINKING THE BIBLE
Inerrancy, Preaching, Inspiration, Authority, Formation, Archaeology, Postmodernism, and More
Richard P. Thompson, Thomas Jay Oord, Editors

Uncontrolling Love
Essays Exploring the Love of God with Introductions by Thomas Jay Oord
Chris Baker, Gloria Coffin, Craig Drurey, Graden Kirksey, Lisa Michaels, Donna Fiser Ward

SACRASAGEPRESS.COM

Made in United States
North Haven, CT
20 November 2022

26981799R00068